The Auldest
Boozers
In Toon

The Auldest Boozers in Toon

Craig Stevenson and John Mackay

Cheapwayround Publishers
East Kilbride

In Memory
of

**Andy Hamilton,
singer, song writer
and all round good guy.**

First Published in 2015 by
Cheapwayround Publishers

ISBN No; 978-0-9570252-5-7

Typeset in East Kilbride by
Cheapwayround Publishers

Printed and Bound by
Bell and Bain Ltd.
Burnfield Road, Thornliebank,
Glasgow, G46 7UQ

Cheapwayround Publishers
22 Balfour Terrace
East Kilbride, G75 0JQ

cheapwayroundpub@yahoo.co.uk
www.cheapwayroundpub.co.uk

By the same authors;

The Cheap Way Round

Still Going

Going Roon the Edge

Inn Aff the Bar

Mud, Sweat and Beers

Contents

Introduction

In our five previous books readers may have detected an overall theme. Namely, using our bus passes to get to various places and have a wee bevy when we get there.

In our defense we have tried to become a little more adventurous. We have gone from aimlessly wandering about the countryside visiting random pubs, see our first two outings, to circumnavigating the entire country, excluding the top left hand side which, according to John, is inhabited by strange people with questionable morals.

After that we took to reporting on the Scottish Football scene, both senior and junior in our fourth and fifth books.

Our latest production has proved even more challenging. It was decided, over a particularly liquid business lunch, that we should produce a book of a more serious and educational nature, but one that would still inform our readers as well as give them ideas for a good day out in our lovely country.

There is an old adage which suggests that if you ever decide to write a book you should stick to what you know best when it comes to subject matter.

Since our main interest and expertise is based in public houses and older ones in particular, it seemed to us that we should use that knowledge to help like-minded people (alkies) to increase their knowledge of Scotland's traditional pubs.

To that end, we decided to search out the oldest pubs and bars in each city and biggish town in Scotland. Along the way we also managed to visit some areas of historical interest

As always we did not take things too seriously, especially John, and if any of the information in the book is not exactly accurate, you can console yourselves in the knowledge that we had a great time gathering it.

In each chapter, we each chose a pub which, in our opinion, could have been the oldest pub in that particular town. We reviewed our pub of choice independently, leaving the other to comment on that choice (in italics)

Craig normally took the first pub in the chapter as he took the whole exercise quite seriously and claimed to care about accuracy of the book.

John, on the other hand, took it upon himself to review the second pub of the day. He was looking for pubs that are also the oldest, just not necessarily in age. Although age was certainly still important, according to John a pub could be the oldest in different ways. Ways, he claims, which he would be able to explain as the chapters unfold. If there was a third pub to be visited in a particular town Craig would then take that one, and so on, until they got a result, or fell down trying.

At the end of the chapter there is a detailed description of how to get to each pub. There are also some fabulous maps at the start of each chapter

All that remains is for the authors to apologise for a bit of an error in judgement which occurred in our last book *Mud, Sweat and Beers*.

The object of that book was to find close rivalries within junior football. We managed to convince ourselves that we had identified the main protagonists in each area of Scotland, but we overlooked an obvious example. Though it has to be said there were others involved in excluding this particular team. In the interests of keeping the peace we shall not name the 'others' involved.

Anyway, we would like to thank the committee of Irvine Victoria JFC for their letter pointing out that they should have been featured in the Ayrshire section of our book.

Aberdeen

John: Scotland's Oil capital was our challenge today. Our aim is to find the oldest pubs, but if, as in Aberdeen, we end up 'well oiled', then so much the better.

As normal with Aberdeen and Inverness, it had to be the 'Gold Bus', one of the great institutions for the 'over 60' traveller.

11

Booking form in hand, we were looking forward to a glorious run up to the North.

Kate and I have friends who live in a wee town called Ellon, which is not too far outside Aberdeen, and who come into the city regularly. I asked Jim (Sandra's man) if he knew anything about old pubs in the Granite City. I didn't expect he would know as he is not a bevy merchant like Craig and me, but he surprised me by answering right away that '*The Grill Bar*' in Union Street was the oldest.

Craig and I had no idea, so this was a starting point on our Aberdeen adventure. We would use our old Scotch tongues from there on. The only problem with using your old Scots tongue in Aberdeen is that the locals use their old Scots tongues, which are completely different from ours. It's all 'fit like the noo' and other local words. Never mind, we're all 'Jock Tamson's Bairns'. No idea what that means either!

There were only two points of interest on our journey from East Kilbride. The first was that our number 18 broke down just before Rutherglen and we all had to get off and wait for the next one. This had us in a panic as we had to get to Buchanan Street in time to catch our G9 Gold Bus which left at 10.10am. Luckily, I had built in time for such an emergency, and after a wee bit of a rush up from George Square, we got our luxury, Double Decker Goldie to Aberdeen.

Needless to say, Craig had something to complain about. There was no hot water for a cup of tea, so we had to make do with a soft drink, scones with butter and jam and tablet, all free. But he still complains.

Before we went to our first pub, we had to deliver some of our previous titles to Waterstone's in Union Street. That task complete, it was on with our story.

As usual, I let Craig have the first choice of the oldest pub in town. He played safe and picked the *The Grill Bar,* even though it was my pal Jim who gave us the information.

Craig's 1ˢᵗ Pub: Scotland's oil capital, Aberdeen, is one of our favourite cities for a good day 'on the lash'. Obviously there are plenty of fine public houses up there well worth a visit. We've been in a fair few already, but on this occasion we were more concerned with history than with mere personal comfort and good beer-honest!

The Grill, Union Street, Aberdeen

I had done a bit of investigating on the internet and discovered that a pub called *The Grill* was reputed to be the oldest in Aberdeen. My investigation could hardly be described as in-depth or conclusive though, since after I found *The Grill* I gave up looking. To some people, and I am thinking mainly of John here, that might sound like laziness, but I had my reasons.

The thing is, we have trusted the information we have found on the net before, only to find out that it was absolute nonsense. My plan was to select only one pub to visit and then just ask the people we met in there where the oldest pub really was. The beauty of this plan was that we would be utilising real local knowledge and I wouldn't be stuck in front of a computer screen all night.

There was an added bonus in choosing to visit *The Grill,* in fact it could be described as an insurance policy. John has friends who either work or live in Aberdeen, and one of these unfortunate people had suggested that he should have a look at The Grill as it was supposed to be the oldest pub in Aberdeen. Even if that turned out to be nonsense, which was always quite likely, I would not have to shoulder all of the blame for picking it.

It is only a ten minute walk from the bus station up to our first pub of the day on Union Street.

The Grill didn't look too great from the outside and I have to admit that we found that quite encouraging. It looked old and rather drab, so you can see why we would be attracted, and in fact it looked like it hadn't been tarted up recently, or indeed ever.

Inside we were delighted to find a right good, old-fashioned Scottish pub. There was a lot of standing room at the extra-long bar. The only tables in the place were small round ones with heavy cast iron legs. These tables were only wide enough to accommodate a couple of pint glasses and possibly a mutton pie if the customer was so inclined. Because of the length of the counter *The Grill* is known as a standing bar. This was obviously a drinking man's pub.

Although *The Grill* is old fashioned it is absolutely spotless. The service we received was also first class. Alison Duncan, our barmaid not only efficiently filled our glasses but filled us in on the pub's history.

The huge gantry is packed solid with bottles of malt whisky. According to Alison there are over 500 different malts up there, some of which are from countries not universally known as malt whisky producers. Although I never touch the stuff myself, that sounded a bit sacrilegious to me but I decided to keep quiet, for once.

Given its name it was not surprising to learn that *The Grill* had originally been a restaurant. It had opened in 1870 and only became a pub in the early 1900s. The bar and the back gantry are made of solid mahogany and would probably be too expensive to

14

recreate nowadays, not to mention being an environmental no-no. A fair chunk of forestry must have been sacrificed to give thirsty Aberdonians something to lean on while knocking back their favourite tipple.

Apparently, when the pub reopened in 1925 after a refurbishment a sign was put in the front window. The sign read ' No Ladies, Please', and it stayed there for the next 50 years. Only the Sex Discrimination Act of 1975 forced the owner to allow women into his bar. It took another 23 years before anyone got round to building a toilet for this new category of customer.
Alison told us that The pub just round the corner still hadn't gotten around to installing any penny spending facilities for the ladies.

The long bar in The Grill

The bar in *The Grill* is reputed to be the longest in Aberdeen. Apparently, its installation caused a bit of a sensation in the city. For some unspecified reason it had to be installed in one piece. This meant removing the windows of the pub and stopping the traffic on Union Street to allow the bar to be slid into place. Only after it was safely inside and the windows had been replaced was it discovered that the bar had been brought in the wrong way round.

I would imagine that the local traders and cart drivers were less than impressed to have to put up with the disruption all over again as the bar was removed, turned around and reinstalled.

Alison and one of The Grill's regulars

Personally I find it reassuring that delivery men and tradesmen in the 1920s were just as clueless as their modern day counterparts. There is no record of who got the blame for this foul-up but, speaking from experience, I would bet that it 'wisnae the gaffer'.

Despite many web sites and various acquaintances of John claiming that the Grill was either the oldest or one of the oldest pubs in Aberdeen, Alison was quite clear that no one from the pub had ever claimed such a distinction. She suggested that there might be some confusion over the age of the building and not the length of time the pub had occupied the site.

Alison also told us that there was an ongoing argument between two nearby pubs about which of them could lay claim to the title of Aberdeen's oldest boozer.

Ma Cameron's and *The Old King's Highway* both claim to have irrefutable proof that they alone deserve the title. Only time and quite a few beers would tell.

Actually there was one other pub which could have been in the running to make the list of pubs we should be visiting. I had accidentally checked out *The Old Blackfriars* on my computer. The pub is on a wee back street, and certainly looked the part.

I got quite excited about the place when I read that the owners had a 'no telly' policy. This was right up our street. Unfortunately, as I read on I discovered that they prided themselves on being a child friendly pub. That got them instantly barred from the list.

John's comments: *Although it was Craig's first pick, I've got to admit that it was a great pub with a long bar. If you want to find it in Union Street, you've got to keep your eyes open.*

Ma Cameron's ghostly entrance

John's 1st pub: We said our farewells and headed out on our quest. Our next port of call was my first choice *Ma Cameron's*. The locals in *The Grill* had told me about a few pubs they thought may be the oldest, but I picked *Ma's* because I liked the name. It's as good a reason as any.

17

Ma's is to be found in Little Belmont Street. This is a nice up-markety area full of shops, bars and Coffee Bars. It's a bit like Rose Street in Edinburgh or the Byres Road area in the West End of Glasgow. Not the sort of area that normally houses the kind of pubs that we like, but I thought that being in Aberdeen, it may be different. We would see!

It was harder finding the bar in the pub than it was finding the pub itself. When you go in the door, you need to take about four rights, three lefts, and two straight ons before you get to the bar. I was dizzy by the time we arrived at the bar, but it's worth the trouble as it's a terrific place.

Ma's is more of a bar that welcomes couples than *The Grill* was. Still, I didn't hold that against it!

The barmaid, Sam Cuthbert, (a female Sam) and the charge hand, Vicky Coull, made us very welcome and set about convincing us that the pub was about 300 years old.

They told us that before the building was a pub, pigs were kept in the building. They also told us that one of its famous customers was none other than Bonnie Prince Charlie. I told them yes, and pigs might fly!

John hunting for spirits

When I asked the girls how they knew for sure that this bar was older than another pub I'd been told about, they said that although that pub may claim to have started earlier, for a period of time it stopped being a bar and selling drink. So that cancels out its claim. The truth will out.

Sam then showed us into the Snug Bar, which is only opened at the weekends. This is part of the original bar and is very atmospheric. Sam told us that, on more than one occasion, she has seen a black ghost, which darts to one side when she opens the door. I believed her as it is a scary wee bar.

She then showed me a brass plaque below one of the windows. On the plaque is engraved 'McNeil's Window'. I asked Sam if this man was famous or had donated money to help the pub develop, or get rid of the smell of the pigs, but no, it was a lot simpler than that. He had caused trouble one night and the barman had thrown him out right through the window. I had never even heard of that happening in Govan! What a place, and old. But was it the oldest? When we said that we should still visit the other pub we had been told about, Sam and Vicky were both adamant that we were wasting our time. *Ma's* was older.

Sam and Vicky

19

We didn't want to upset the girls, but the quest had to continue. We said our farewells to another brilliant Aberdeen institution, and following Sam's instructions, made our way along a couple of streets, down about a thousand stairs, and into the other pub we had been told about; *The Kings Highway.*

Craig's comments: Liked this place a lot. Maybe just a wee bit on the pretentious side for me, or maybe it's me who's being pretentious.

Craig's 2nd Pub: *The Old Kings Highway* is just off Union Street, down a very steep flight of steps. John was amazed that I could navigate my way to this pub without so much as a glance at the map. I told him that it was nothing special, simply a talent that few men could ever hope to emulate.

The truth is, however, that we have actually been to this pub before. Obviously John was either drunk at the time or his memory has finally packed in. Either explanation seems reasonable.

The Highway is situated in a very impressive-looking building, and the interior is quite impressive as well. It is very clean and tidy but is a wee bit more modern than you might expect.

On the road to the 'Highway'

Our barmaid served up our drinks and stayed to chat to us. She was quite adamant that the *Old King's Highway* was indeed the oldest pub in Aberdeen. It would seem that the owner of the pub eventually got tired of listening to his customers arguing about which pub in Aberdeen really was the oldest, so he took it upon himself to go through all the historical records in an attempt to prove his case.

While we were chatting to the barmaid, Jenny McLennan, the owner, Jack (real name John Durham), actually phoned the pub. After a minute or two Jenny told him that we were in the bar and asking questions about the age of his pub. In a three-way conversation we were told that, during his search of records, he had found definitive proof that his place was the oldest. In fact he had taken copies of the records round to the owners of *Ma Cameron's* and got them to concede that the title was his.

So far we have yet to see any of that proof and the staff round at *Ma Cameron's,* seem blissfully unaware that any such proof exists.

The facts as told to us are that Ma's was established in 1747, while *The Old Kings Highway* claims to have been doing business since 1741. On the face of it *The Highway* takes the title, but in historical terms, only just.

Of course nothing is ever simple in the pub trade. A number of people have pointed out that to claim the title of the oldest pub some of the original structure should still be evident. *The Highway* is now what is called a Gastro pub and is therefore no longer a real public house.

We decided not to get involved in any further argument and changed the subject. Being a very old building, we asked Jenny if the pub ever had any visitors from the great beyond. Actually I don't think we've ever been to a pub yet that doesn't have at least one malevolent spirit rumbling about the bar making the lights flicker and clinking glasses. The Highway was no exception, in fact Jenny herself claims to have seen a dark menacing spirit. John suggested that maybe the spirit in question was Dark Rum, but Jenny insisted that what she had seen was the pub ghost.

It seems that sightings have been so frequent that a group of ghost hunters have visited the pub to check it for apparitions. One of the customers happened to mention that a film of their endeavours can be seen on YouTube. I couldn't resist it. It was fifteen minutes of pure, unadulterated, pish.

Their investigation, unsurprisingly, began dead on midnight, down in the cellar. The fearless ghost hunters then spent the rest of the night filming absolutely nothing, in HD.

Jenny and John (the Letch)

Back in the real world, we enjoyed our time in *The Old King's Highway*. The beer was excellent as was the service. The pub itself was very comfortable. It may well be the oldest pub in town, but it certainly doesn't show its age in its decor. Unlike *The Grill* and *Ma Cameron's* this pub has chosen to move with the times. It doesn't trade on its heritage which could be seen as a refreshing change.

But, as we accumulate evermore heritage ourselves, I have to say that we both appreciate the more traditional pub which has a few objects sitting around the place which are older than we are.

As things stand I would have to say that *The Old King's Highway* is possibly the oldest pub in town, but I'm sure there will be a few Aberdonians out there who will disagree with me.

John's comments: *We have visited three bars today, and all are great in different ways. Which one is the oldest, and does anybody care? It's a toss-up between 'Ma's' and 'The King's'. 'The Grill' admitted it was not in the running, although a lot of information on the Web states that it is. That is why we travel to these pubs ourselves to get the truth from the Horses', or Pigs', mouths. I believe all our readers should head up to Aberdeen on the Gold Bus and find out for themselves. They won't be disappointed.*

John: We left *The Kings,* and headed for the Bus Station. As is our wont, we had left some time up our sleeve so we could have a quick couple in *The Spirit Level,* our favourite bar in the city. Julie was there to give us a warm welcome and we ended our trip to Aberdeen feeling no pain. The bus journey home went by in a flash as we slept all the way.

So ended a great day out in Aberdeen. Which is the oldest pub? Make up your own mind; they're all great.

Find oor Auld Boozers

by Bus . . . .

The Gold Bus from Buchanan Street Bus Station, non-stop, right into Aberdeen Bus Station. There is a bus every hour or so, but most of them take a bit of time as they go through other towns like Perth and Dundee, so check the time of the Gold Bus, and book a seat, it is only 50p.

. . . . then by Boot

The Grill bar
The Grill Bar is found by turning left out of the bus station and walking up the hill to Union Street. Turn left and you will find it no bother. It doesn't claim to be the oldest, but it has the longest bar I have ever seen and the pub is definitely worth a visit, more of a man's pub than the other two we visited.

Ma Cameron's
Ma Cameron's, turn right when you leave *The Grill*, walk over the bridge, turn left and then right and it's on your left on Little Belmont Street. One of the two that claim to be the oldest. It's a great bar, but behave yourself or you might end up going through a window.

The King's Highway
The Kings Highway, go back down onto Union Street, cross the road and go down a thousand stairs and it is in front of you, you can't miss it. Another of the two pubs that claim to be the oldest. The main thing is that, like the two above, it is a great bar and they all should be visited.

Perth

John: In the heart of Scotland, one of our richest farming areas, and where you find farmers and farm workers, there are bound to be pubs, and good ones at that. Hopefully they would be old as well.

I played safe and booked us places on both journeys. That's £1 I'll never see again! Our bus was leaving at 11.00am so we were at Buchanan Street in time to nick into the wee Sainsbury's beside the bus station for a paper and snashter's to eat on the bus. No free tea and sandwiches like you get on the Gold Bus.

The bus was fairly empty and Craig picked us seats right at the emergency exit. The door was in front of us so we had acres of leg room. We had just sat down when Craig said he didn't like the big space in front of us, so we got up to move to a seat further back. As we stood up a woman opposite stood up and said she would take our seats as it would let her 'spread her legs'. 'Do you not mean stretch', I asked. She was dead embarrassed but had a great laugh. At my age a cup of tea and a scone are excitement enough on any bus trip.

It's a lovely run up to Perth, the sun was shining and the forecast was for it to be a very warm day. How often do you hear that in Scotland?

Stirling Castle, the Wallace Monument, home of the Sword of Wallace, Bannockburn, home of the Bruce, Dunblane, home of the Andy Murray and Gleneagles, home of the rich dudes are just some of the interesting places you pass on the way.

As usual Craig had used one of his magic phones and found a few pubs claiming to be the oldest. He had picked one which he said looked like a shoe-in for the oldest, so we should go there first. I said that I would just talk to a local in the pub and get the gist on what is the real oldest pub.

As you all know, if you have read our previous books, I usually phone the local Waterstones, if there is one, to ask if they need any books. It helps to cover our bevy costs if we can sell some books while we are in the area. Perth is not one of our top selling shops, so you could have knocked me off my bar stool with a coaster when they ordered 20 books. Shucks, jings and for any favour were something like my comments to Craig when I got the order. The only downside is that we had 20 books to hump up to Perth, so the first thing we did when we got off the bus was to wander round to Waterstone's and deliver them.

Books delivered, we made our way to Craig's first choice of old pubs.

Craig's 1St Pub: *The Old Ship Inn;* Initially I just couldn't put my finger on what was so different about our journey up to Perth. Eventually it hit me: at no time was the landscape blotted out by torrential rain. It turned out that the temperature in Perth and Kinross that day was the highest in Britain at 27°C. It had all the makings of a good drinking day.

Once again I used my superior navigating skills to get us quickly to our first stop of the day, *The Old Ship Inn.*

We drop anchor at The Old Ship

Although The Ship's address is 31 High Street I happened to know that it wasn't actually on High Street, it is on Skinnergate. For some reason I had forgotten to tell John this little bit of information. As we walked along High Street, with no sign of the pub, he was getting more and more agitated. Phrases like 'I might have known' and 'you useless B' became more frequent as it

27

looked, from his point of view, as if I had buggered things up yet again.

With perfect comic timing he managed to stop directly opposite the Skinnergate to tell me what he thought of my performance as a pub finder. It was reminiscent of a bad pantomime when he demanded to know where the pub was and I answered 'it's behind you'. He was speechless with gratitude.

The Old Ship Inn is generally accepted to be one of, if not the, oldest pubs in Perth.

Although the outside of the pub has changed very little over the years it is still surprisingly modern looking. The original building dates from 1665 and unlike most pubs which seem to change names almost as often as they change owners, *The Ship* has kept its original name down through the ages.

The ancient mariner gets nostalgic

28

The name of the street, Skinnergate obviously relates to the animal hides which were shipped into Perth to feed the growing leather goods trade. Back in mediaeval times, cargoes were unloaded at quay a on the River Tay, which is just along from the Skinnergate, at the end of High Street.

Legend has it that in 1746 Bonnie Prince Charlie visited the town and made a declaration at the old market cross, not too far from T*he Ship*. Legend also has it that Charlie liked the odd beverage or two, so it seems a fair bet that he might have popped into the lounge bar for a swift one before trying to rally his troops for the imminent invasion of England.

I certainly find a bit of a session helps loosen the old vocal chords. Anyway I liked the look of this pub as soon as I clapped eyes on it. Inside it was even better. It is well laid out with an open plan bar and a lounge area. The decor is just spot on for the likes of me and John, good clean surroundings, barstools and only one television up on the wall. The lounge area, technically part of the same room, is a smashing wee, quiet place, where, if you like that sort of thing, you can sit and chat to friends without being drowned out by the usual bar noise we are subjected to nowadays.

Jim and Tina, 'The Old Ships crew

29

Our barman, Jim Collins, spotted us coming in and was over asking us what we wanted even before I managed to collapse onto a well upholstered barstool. We like service like that

We were the only customers in the bar although there were a few people sitting outside taking advantage of the sunshine, or as I call it, risking skin cancer. Stay inside, stay near the bar, stay healthy that's what I say.

Apparently there were some 'suits' from Belhaven Brewery in the pub checking up on the place. They were in the lounge talking to Tina, the gaffer.

As soon as he heard this John started talking in stage whispers, extolling the virtues of Belhaven's various products. I knew what he was up to straight away.

At most, he was looking for a bit of sponsorship for future books, and at the very least he was angling for a free drink. Neither of these two options was forthcoming.

Tina came over to join us at the bar and between the four of us we had a great half hour of daft pub chat. We told Tina how much we liked her pub and urged her to keep it just as it was, friendly and for the most part child free.

I got the impression that she liked a laugh, so when she said she had to leave as she had an appointment to get her hair dyed purple I thought she was having us on. Not so. Hopefully we will return to *The Old Ship* someday soon, just so that we can get a picture of a Perthshire purple pint-pulling patron.

While we were talking about the history of the pub somebody mentioned that The Ship was once the haunt of travelling actors and musicians. Given that back in olden days such people were often regarded as on a par with tramps and prostitutes I suggested that maybe that's one claim to fame best left out of their Facebook page.

Jim had been keeping us entertained with a few daft stories and when we mentioned trying to find another contender for the oldest pub title he immediately suggested that we should try *Blackfriars*, round on South Street. Of course he didn't think it was

30

older than *The Ship,* but he said that it was the kind of pub he thought we would like.

Usually that's the kind of patter people use to get shot of us, but I prefer to think that Jim is one of the good guys and really did know we would appreciate a nice wee pub. He even came round from behind the bar to show us the quickest way to our next stop.

He had tried explaining the route to John but he was at the stage where right and left had started to sound like a complicated maths equation.

John's comments; *Craig's first pick was a great one.* The Old Ship *is one of the best pubs we have visited and the barman was good company. No complaints from me about the old date or the pub itself.*

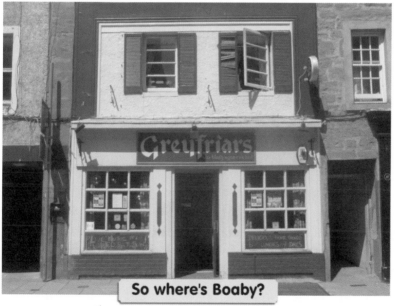

So where's Boaby?

John's 1ˢᵗ Pub: *Greyfriars.* Sausage Rolls in hand, we walked round the corner into South Street and found our next pub, *Greyfriars.* This is a tiny wee pub, but has a great atmosphere and

31

we were immediately made to feel at home by the owner, Pauline Marshall, and the barmaid, Alba Bernardis. I immediately thought she must be a Gaelic Orphan, but she is Pauline's daughter and is married to an Italian. I know it was still early in the day, but a fair amount bevy had been downed so I hope my memory is to the fore about the names and relationships.

Pauline and Alba

The girls and three great locals, Ken, Marjorie and Jim, filled us in with details of the history of this great bar.

Their first claim was that it started in the fifteen hundreds, but there is no written proof. Mind you, it must be pretty old as it started life as *The Brown Cow,* then it was *The Drovers,* then in the 50s and 60s it was *The Ewe and Lamb.* This name was changed to the present *Greyfriars* because the locals called it *The Screw and Scram*, the name summing up what went on in it. It's called *Greyfriars* because the area it's in used to be Greyfriars Graveyard. Mind you, if it used to be a graveyard, it must still be there unless they built over the bodies. I'll have to check.

Ken, Jim, Marjorie, Alba and two others

I reckon this pub has a claim to be the oldest small pub with a low ceiling in Perth. That's good enough for me.

Craig's comments: The only problem I had with this pub was the fact that part of my memory of it had somehow been erased. I have no idea how that happened but I do remember laughing and chatting with the staff and customers.

I will definitely be going back there. Maybe someone in the place can tell me what I got up to the last time.

Craig's 2nd Pub: We were having such fun in *Greyfriars* that we didn't really want to leave, but we needed to visit one more pub on our quest to find Perth's oldest bar.

Somehow we settled on a compromise: we would still leave *Greyfriar's*, but we would take the bar crowd with us. It sounds completely insane but, at the time, it seemed quite reasonable to us. It certainly made for a fun-filled visit.

The Salutation Hotel didn't really fit in with the boozer description, but it does have a lot of history on its side. As soon as we stepped through the front door it was obvious that we were well out of our comfort zone. I would estimate that there is more Axminster carpet in this place than any other building in Scotland.

I was fully expecting to be redirected to the tradesman's entrance at any moment. When I found out how much they charged for their booze I thought that might have been a better option. It also explained why there was no sign of any wear and tear on the carpet around the bar.

We can't say we weren't warned that the Salutation was a bit of a step up from our usual run-of-the-mill pub, but I don't think we were quite ready for what we found there.

Perhaps if we had known that the guest list of former clientele included the likes of Boris Johnson we might have checked out another watering hole. Even John knew that old Boris wasn't known for slumming it.

Our barman, Andy Clark, was keen to show me around the hotel and I have to admit it was very impressive. For example, the corridors were wider than my house. Andy led me on a tour of some of the function rooms, each one bigger than the one before. On the way back to the bar we stopped to take a look at the display of famous former customers. With the exception of some allegedly famous jockeys I think I recognised everyone on the board. There were pictures of some world renowned entertainers and politicians,

Andy says hello from 'The Salutation'

We re-joined the drinkers in the bar and I slowly drank my half pint of larger. The reason I had ordered a half pint was not because I had been overcome by a sudden bout of sophistication, but rather I didn't want John to choke to death when he heard how much a full pint would have cost.

We finished our drinks and waded through the thick piled carpet over to the door then out and back across to *Greyfriars* for a reasonably priced final drink, or two.

Eventually it was time to make our way back to the bus station, but not before stopping for chips. While we were in the shop one of us, I don't know who, suggested that we should buy some chocolate for the bus.

The only reason I remember the chocolate incident is that the next morning, while getting ready to go out, I found a large misshaped brick of Cadburys Dairy Milk welded to the inside pocket of my good jacket.

John's comments; This was one of the most old fashioned places I have ever been in. I'm 68, I think, and I reckon I must be one of the youngest customers they have had in years. The barman, Andy was great company and his stories of famous guests were priceless.

John; We bought a couple of bags of chips and had finished them by the time our M8 bus turned up to take us back to Glasgow.

The first two pubs we visited were great and are a must if you are ever in Perth. The Hotel, well, as my Granny used to say, 'if you can't say something nice about a place' don't say anything. The barman, Andy Clark, was an ok guy though.

Which bar is the oldest? probably *The Old Ship*, and a better bar you'll be hard pressed to find.

Find oor Auld Boozers

by Bus . . . .

The M8-Buchanan Street Bus Station, non-stop, into Perth Bus Station. Bus goes through Cumbernauld, Stirling and Dunblane.

. . . . then by Boot

The Old Ship Inn
For '*The Old Ship*', Leave the bus station, go down to South Street, walk along in the direction of the river, and up into High Street. The bar is in The Skinnergate, which is at number 31 High Street.

Greyfriars
'*Greyfriars*' is on South Street, along near the river on the left hand side as you look towards the river.

The Salutation Hotel
The Salutation Hotel is across the road from 'Greyfriars' on South Street.

Dumfries

John: Dumfries, the home of our national bard, the great Robert Burns, from the age of 29 until his death. I wanted to include some history into this chapter as we are trying to find old pubs, and Burns was known to enjoy a few beers with his mates long ago.

Our trip today has an actual link with Burns as he was known to enjoy a wee bevy in *'The Globe Inn'*, which claims to be the oldest pub in Dumfries, established in 1610. We are going to try our best to confirm this, or get pissed in the attempt.

Although our bus to Dumfries, the old X74, leaves from Glasgow, we picked it up in Hamilton. This saves us at least two pints, or 40 minutes in real time. We had a wee fright when our No. 201 bus to Hamilton was hit by a council lorry before it even got down to the EK bus station. Names and addresses were taken, but nobody was injured and we were soon on our way.

We arrived in historic Dumfries in bright sunshine, and after delivering some of our books to the local Waterstone's, wandered across the High Street, up a wee lane and into the unbelievably atmospheric *Globe Inn* which of course houses 'Burn's Howff', the room he liked best.

Craig had already checked the web and knew that *The Globe* had a big claim to be the oldest, so he claimed it for his first pub in Dumfries. I agreed. Anything for a quiet life.

Craig's 1st pub: *The Globe:* After more than 20 minutes or so of intense Internet-based research I had identified Dumfries' oldest pub, the only problem being I didn't believe it. That wasn't a great start to our day out down South.

The pub in question was *The Globe* and we had visited it a couple of years ago. It was a really good pub and we had enjoyed our visit. But the thing was, I was absolutely certain that it wasn't the oldest pub in town. However since even I cannot claim to be correct 100 per cent of the time, I was willing to go back there and investigate. Fortunately for us, and this book, there was more to the story of the Dumfries' oldest pub than met the eye.

Once again we had combined our day out with a spot of book delivering. Waterstone's in Dumfries had requested a resupply of our highly successful scribblings, and we duly delivered them, before setting off for our first pint of the day.

As usual there was a bit of banter with the girls in the bookshop, and it was while we were chatting that I heard something that saved me from making a complete arse of myself. One of the girls asked us where we were off to, I said that we were about to make the long trek over the river to find the oldest pub in Dumfries. She looked a bit confused and then said that if that was the case, why were we not going to *The Globe*.

There was obviously something wrong. I did notice that when she mentioned *The Globe* she was pointing in exactly the opposite direction to the pub I was talking about.

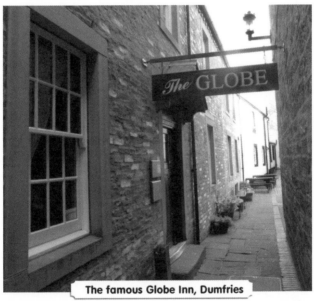

The famous Globe Inn, Dumfries

To cut a long story short, it turns out that there are two pubs in Dumfries called *The Globe*. To my mind that is just bizarre, but nobody we met down there seemed to think it was in any way unusual. And so, instead of a half mile hike to our first pub of the day, we simply wandered across the road from the shop.

As soon as I saw the entrance to *The Globe* I knew we were onto a winner, and not just because the sign above the close announced that the pub was established in 1610.

The actual front entrance is about 20 yards along the alley from the High Street and is exactly what you would expect of a building of that age. There has been very little done to change the decor in most areas of the pub in recent times. In fact almost everywhere you turn is a photo opportunity.

We decided to start our day in the Snug Bar. It is very atmospheric with photographs paintings and framed poetry all around the walls. In fact up until the barmaid came into the room, we were the youngest things in there.

As you can imagine we have met more than a few barmaids in our day and the best of these are the ones who really enjoy their work. In *The Globe* not only did the girls, Cathy Morton and Jane Brown enjoy working there, they were extremely proud of the place.

John with Cathy and Jane

The connection with Robert Burns means that *The Globe* sees a constant flow of tourists eager to take in the atmosphere of one of his favourite watering holes. There is Burns memorabilia absolutely everywhere. Cathy suggested that we might like a wee tour of the pub. I thought she meant the dining room and such like, but there was so much more to see. The gaffer, Jane, offered to be our guide and off we went. She certainly knew her stuff and I was just about to say something to that effect when I overhead her telling John that she was actually the President of the Robert Burns World Federation. I decided to keep my mouth shut.

Upstairs we were shown the bed that Burns sometimes slept off the odd heavy night of poetry recitation. Everywhere we turned there was some artefact associated with Burns which collectors would pay a fortune to own. Despite being an Ayrshire man I have to confess that I have never been a Burns man, but even I was amazed to see how well conserved all these items were.

But Jane wasn't finished amazing us. She pointed to the windows, and at first I thought she meant to show me something outside. It turned out that it was the windows themselves she wanted us to look at. It is not often that I am stuck for words, but this was one of these times. Actually I could feel the hairs on the back of my neck standing up. Scratched onto the glass of the windows were several lines of poetry. They had been etched there by Robert Burns himself.

Jane wastes her breath trying to educate John

Back down stairs we were shown into the 'Howff', the tiny drinking den used by Burns. Next to the fireplace in there is a wooden backed chair in which the great man used to sit while regaling the punters with his poetry and stories. I'm happy to say I was allowed to sit in the chair for a few minutes.

I was still sitting there when Jane said she would buy us both a drink if we could recite a verse form one of the Bards poems. It was a bit of a stretch, but I managed to remember a single verse from my school days. I'm still waiting for my pint, Jane.

Back in the Snug Bar we settled down for a wee drinking session in memory of the great man, a renowned drinker in his own right. As ever with old buildings, and old pubs in particular, the talk soon got round to ghost stories. And The Globe has its fair share of such stories.

Rabbie's bed, enough said!

It has never been suggested that the ghost in question is that of Burns himself, but the girls behind the bar insist there is a spirit which wanders around the pub causing trouble. On one occasion the ghost made its presence felt while a Burns supper was taking

42

place in the building. The piper, a retired police sergeant, was standing at the top of the stairs getting ready for his entrance when suddenly he was hauled backwards onto the landing. By all accounts the sergeant was a chunky chap, not easily shifted. I suppose you could say there were strong spirits involved.

On another occasion a television crew was filming a documentary in *The Globe* when the apparition made an appearance. It seems there was a lot of screaming and howling, none of which came from the ghost.

While chatting to the girl, the subject of home towns came up. We expected to hear that they were both Dumfries born and bred, but that was not the case. It seems that Cathy is originally from Govan. That got John all excited. He told them that he too was from Govan, the posh end of course.

That got the biggest laugh of the day, as Cathy put it, 'Now we know you're a blether, there is nae posh end in Govan'. With his credibility in tatters we finished our drinks and prepared to leave for John's choice of pub.

Just before we left I thought that I should bring up the subject of the possible confusion caused by two pubs sharing the same name. One of the girls told me that they often get each other's mail and regularly have to send someone round to exchange it. It seems unlikely that the other pub will ever change its name so this will continue to happen.

I just wonder how often drinkers get into trouble because of the name mix-up. Meeting up with friends could be problematic if you choose the wrong one, and establishing a decent alibi could be decidedly dodgy.

Anyway, whether you are a fan of our national bard, a keen historian or just enjoy a good drink in great surroundings, I recommend you visit *The Globe*. Just make sure it's the right one.

John's comments: *Cannot make any derogatory remarks about Craig's first pub as I liked it as much as he did. A must if you are ever in Dumfries and especially if you are a Burns fan.*

John's 1ˢᵗ Pub: *The Hole I' the Wa;* Following the instructions I got from a wee man in *The Globe*, we turned right when we got out, and went along the main street. I think the pub was also in The High Street, *'The Hole I' the Wa'*. I did a double take before I realized that this was the pub I was looking for. I thought it was called *The Hole in the Wall*. I've got to be honest and admit my Burn's talk is not as good as Jane Brown's.

"Dae a really have to go in here?"

'The Wa', as I'll now call it, also has an atmospheric entrance up a wee close, but there the atmosphere definitely stops. There is nothing wrong with the pub if you like a modern place and all the trimmings. But although it does date back to 1620, it was not to our taste. Having said all that, there is nothing wrong with the place, the barman was friendly and it is a very popular bar in the town. We only had one drink and left to find another old pub that Craig had heard about from someone at the bar.

Craig's comments: There is nothing wrong with The Hole I' the Wa'. *For people who like a bright noisy place to eat or drink it is probably ideal. I can't stand the place. To be honest I would rather give up beer than have to do my drinking in this pub.*

If there had been any doubt in my mind about this pub, the squawking tanoy telling the hungry masses that their meal was ready just underlined my first impression.

Craig's 2nd Pub: *The Tam-o'-Shanter.* Why would you name your pub after the bunnet? asked John. I think he was kidding actually, but you never can tell. *The Tam-o'-Shanter* on Queensbury Street was not a pub I had intended to choose for today's visit. It chose itself in a way. We got off the bus a stop before Whitesands, where the bus station is.

Since we were carrying books to deliver to Waterstones shop I thought we could cut down on the walking by getting off the bus early and walking through the back streets to the pedestrian area of the High Street. While we were doing this we stumbled on the Tam-o'-Shanter.

I thought it looked great and decided that it would be my second choice pub, and that's where we headed as soon as we escaped from *The Hole I' the Wa'*.

The famous Tam O Shanter Inn

Being on a sort of backstreet I had expected the pub to be a lot darker than it was. But the interior was very bright and welcoming. We felt really at home and in no time at all we got chatting to the barmaid and she told me that *The Tam O'Shanter* was originally a coaching inn and had first opened its doors in 1630 I was amazed. Somehow we had managed not only to find the oldest pubs in Dumfries but had managed to visit them in the correct order, *the Globe:* 1610; *The Hole I' the Wa':* 1620; and now *The Tam-o'-Shanter:* 1630.

To the outsider it probably looked like we professionally researched our subject, pouring over numerous history books, endlessly scouring the internet, just to make sure we got everything spot on. That's nonsense of course, we just struck it lucky.

Ghostbusters

The Tam-o'-Shanter sits on Queensbury Street and its position means that for the most part its clientele is made up mainly of locals.

When we found out that the pub didn't have a single television or even a jukebox John immediately demanded political asylum. But changed his mind just as quickly when we were told that folk music was the preferred form of entertainment in the pub.

Apart from the bar there is a small snug and a back room. I noticed that there were some of those old fashioned hand pull pumps on the bar, and I have to say they really added to the authentic look of the place. Not that I was likely to be drinking anything that came out of them. I'm not a fan of real ale. The one time I did try it I thought someone had swapped my beer for a pint of silage run-off.

While we were having a laugh with the barmaid, I mentioned the ghost story we had been told round at the globe. Not to be outdone she said that her pub had its very own spirit. She told us that when she was young, she had come into contact with the ghost late one night when she was on her own tidying up the bar. She didn't seem over keen to share her story with us. The story suggested that she had been traumatised by her ordeal. Eventually, after a lot of pleading by John she was persuaded to come round to the front of the bar and share her scary story.

It is part of her job to clear up the bar after the last customer has left for the night. As usual she had her personal music player belting out her favourite tunes while she worked. Between wiping down tables and sweeping the floor she was in the habit of dancing along with the music. While getting really energetic to one particular song, she suddenly became aware of someone or something standing at her shoulder, she actually feel the breath of this entity on her neck.

Completely spooked she let out a scream and rushed out of the pub as fast as she possibly could. She didn't stop running, or screaming, until she reached the managers' front door, several streets away. After calming down, both of them returned to the pub.

In her haste to get as far away as possible from the heavy breather, she had left the pub doors lying wide open. Both girls quickly checked the premises, and finding no sign of any of any visitors, from this or any other world, the manager replayed the CCTV tape. By this time John, who had been holding his breath, was on the point of turning blue. As it turned out there was nothing on the tape, that is to say, nothing other than a very clear picture of barmaid, dancing like a loony.

We wondered why she would be traumatised by this non-encounter with the pub ghost, but apparently that's not what affected her. The real trauma came the next morning when she returned to the pub to do her shift. When she walked into the pub she found her customers falling about laughing while watching her performance up on the TV screen. I think it was played for the rest of the day on a loop.

The rest of our visit to *Tam-o'-Shanters* followed a similar path, the customers told us daft stories and we laughed our heads off. It's a really nice way to spend an afternoon. I fully recommend it.

John's comments: It's a bad day for me as far as slagging off Craig's pubs. The two he picked were great. So credit where it's due, his two were better than my one. Mind you, if you're young and enjoy a lively night out, 'The Wa' would probably be more to your liking. You have to remember our tastes tend towards the old and traditional.

John: The sun was still splitting the coconuts as we walked down to the river to sit and enjoy our pieces, I was back on the Corned Beef and English Mustard. We still had half an hour to kill before our bus home so we went across the road into the nearest bar, can't even remember its name. We had a quick one and then got our bus back to Hamilton. I think we slept the whole way back as the journey seemed to last about five minutes.

So ended a great day in Dumfries, home not only of our national Bard, but one of the oldest pubs in all Scotland. Only time will tell.

Find oor Auld Boozers

by Bus . . . .

The X74 direct from Buchanan Street Bus Station will get you there in a couple of hours. It stops at Hamilton, Lesmahagow and Moffat on the way.

. . . . then by Boot

The Globe Inn

The Globe Inn is in the High Street. You get off the bus at the terminus by the river, turn left and walk up the road to the High Street, it is only a couple of minutes.

Definitely the oldest in Dumfries and one of the best bars we have ever visited.

The Hole I' the Wa'

The Hole I' the Wa' is also in High Street and easy to find.

An old pub, not the oldest and not to our liking, but still a good bar for food and drink.

Tam O' Shanter

The Tam O' Shanter is in a wee street called Queensbury Street, just behind High Street, almost directly behind 'The Hole I' the Wa' .

The Tam is the third oldest by date, but our second favourite in Dumfries, definitely worth a visit.

Inverness

John: We love going to Inverness, or anywhere for that matter with bars. It's also a beautiful run up the A9 on the Gold Bus where luxury and free tea and pieces abound, not to mention tablet, not that there was any mention of it on the bus either, but more of that in a minute.

Our Highland Capital is a lovely city. We have visited it many times on our travels and have never been disappointed with the hospitality in the many pubs we have sampled.

Today, we had a more specific aim: to find the oldest pub in town. Now remember, we cannot be held responsible for information concerning the age of pubs we report on. In fact, we cannot be held responsible for very much at our age!

Our bus into Glasgow was delayed and we had to run up from George Square to the Bus Station. By the time we got to the bus I was knackered, Craig was worse than knackered, but I'm not allowed to use the word that would describe how he felt, though most of you know what it is.

The Gold Bus was packed, and there were only two seats left, luckily they were opposite each other, Craig was smart and dived into the empty one; the one opposite had a women sitting in the aisle seat and all her bags were in the window seat. What is it about people like that! They can see the bus is packed but they just don't give a shit. Luckily the wee man in charge of the free teas was on the ball and told her to move her bags. She was none too chuffed. We had a wee chat later and she was all right. Thought I'd mention this just in case she reads the book.

Craig was in one of his complaining moods. They are getting more common recently. Today it was that the water for our tea was cold by the time we got it, there was no tablet, and we were only offered water instead of a selection of soft drinks after our tea and scone. These things we get are all free for goodness sake, but he still complains. He says he is going to downgrade the Gold Bus, but all I can say is that it is a brilliant service, or as Burns would say,

'Lang may your'e tred grip the tarmac'

We fairly belted up the A9 and in what seemed like no time at all we were in Inverness and the sun was shining.

As I've said before, it would be easy for us to use the Web to find the pubs and the details about them, but we want to talk to the locals and come up with our own conclusions, even if the information is not of an encyclopedic standard.

That's not to say Craig didn't have a wee look on the Web, as he has to find the first pub to visit, but he assured me it was only a wee look. He picked one that he said had most claims to be the oldest. As always, our intention is to weed out the imposters and find the genuine oldest, or get pissed trying.

As usual, Craig gets the first choice of which pub he thinks is the oldest. As you should know by now, he is more interested in finding the oldest pub by recorded date, whereas I'm not too bothered about the actual date. I'm more interested in it being the oldest pub in town for some other reason; what that reason is will vary. For all I know, sometimes it might even be the date!

Craigs 1st Pub: *Gellions* was my first choice of pub to visit in Inverness. Not because it is my favourite or even because my extensive research suggested it was the oldest pub in the city. The reason I chose it was quite simple. It was the handiest.

After delivering our books to the shop in the centre we simply wandered along the road and down the hill to the pub. We had been in this pub before on one of our earlier adventures, and to be perfectly honest we hadn't liked it very much. But such is our commitment to our work that we were prepared to suffer another boring half an hour in a place we had vowed never to return to.

I'm really glad we did. Everything had changed since our last visit. This time around we were not ignored by the bar staff. The bar was comfortable and the beer was just right. As far as I could tell the whole place had been gutted and remodelled. It actually looks like a proper pub now and nothing like the cafe-themed nonsense it once was. I can only assume that the former bar staff have moved on to careers better suited to their talents, such as working part-time behind the checkout counter in Poundshop.

Our barmaid, Siwar Louati, was very pleasant and helpful, even though she was quite busy. She did confirm our belief that *Gellions* is the oldest pub in Inverness.

Siwar told us that local legend had it that the great William Topaz McGonagall, John's favourite poet, had stayed in lodgings quite nearby. There is no official record of this visit, not even a few really bad verses of poetry. Robert Burns also stayed locally and, given his well-known liking for a wee refreshment and a bit of bar banter, it is quite likely that he might have wandered into some nearby Inn of an evening. Many of the buildings which date from his time have long since been demolished. Possibly due to Inverness's seemingly endless programme of bridge building.

Siwar gives us the low down on Gellions history

Siwar told me that there is supposed to be a tunnel leading from the castle to cellar of *The Gellions*. Usually I would take this local knowledge with a pinch of salt but there is maybe a grain of truth to this particular legend. It would seem that Mary Queen of Scots once turned up at Inverness castle seeking shelter. Unfortunately, for Mary, the castle governor was not a fan, and told her to keep moving. Luckily, Mary managed to secure a couple of nights B&B just along the road from where the pub now stands. Someone, it might have been me, suggested that Mary

54

could well have been mooching around the cellar, possibly looking for a decent bottle of French wine, when she discovered the secret tunnel. The Queen and her troops could well have used the tunnel to make an unexpected appearance up at the castle.

It is certainly true that Mary and her troops forcibly entered the castle. Not known for her forgiving nature Mary had the old governor executed as soon as she got settled in.

I'm not sure how historically accurate all of this account of the capture of Inverness Castle is. To be honest, we had polished off a few beers before putting pen to paper on this page of Scottish history, and I may have gotten a bit carried away with the whole thing.

According to my research Gellions has been in business since 1841. Before that time the building contained Inverness burgh Court. I was a bit disappointed by this piece of knowledge as I had imagined that the pub was much older. We had heard all the stories about Mary Queen of Scots and the castle tunnel and had assumed that there was a historical connection between it and *Gellions*. But not only was the pub not in existence at that time, but the present castle wasn't built until 1836, the original one having been destroyed by the Jackobite army in 1746.

We asked Siwar if she could tell us about any other pubs in the town which might have a claim to the oldest pub title. She mentioned the usual suspects, *Blackfriars, the Phoenix* etcetera, but she also asked if we had ever visited the *Back Bar* in *Gellions*. It is a totally separate bar, but it is still part of the main pub. A customer who was sitting just up from me must have been listening as he warned us that this bar, also known as *Monty's*, was a bit on the rough side.

That sealed it for me; we were definitely going to visit it, although that was easier said than done. There is a lane down the side of *Gellions* and we could see a couple of worthies sitting outside having a smoke. But the gate to the lane was shut. Just for a minute it gave the impression that we were looking into a cage.

Now I'm not trying to suggest that the clientele of *Monty's* needed caging in, but a couple of them did appear to have gone a bit feral. Anyway, we walked around the corner into Church Street and found another entrance to the *Back Bar*.

I think it would be fair to say that *Monty's* has successfully resisted any attempts at modernisation for quite a few years. I don't know who is to blame for this, but I would like to offer my thanks to them. We have seen many, many pubs, while out on your travels but I have to say *Monty's* is the one we felt most instantly at home in.

It is quite a small bar and on the day we visited it was fairly busy. I can honestly say that every person in there qualified for the title of unique character, including the barman who turned out to be Monty himself.

To the uninitiated the roaring shouting and more than a little swearing of the guys playing dominoes at the bar could probably sound very threatening. However nothing could be further from the truth, as we eventually found out. We were having a ball, or perhaps' bawl' might better explain the sound being produced in there.

Monty and the gang in the back bar

We stayed in there for a few pints, just to soak up the atmosphere you understand, and enjoyed some great pub banter.

One of the guys told us about the pub ghost who apparently turns up and throws pint glasses around a bar. I've been in lots of pubs like that and trouble is almost always caused by spirits.

Come to think of it, I have witnessed a few miraculous happenings in pubs in my time. Many years ago I used to drink in a pub where this blind man could somehow sense when a pint had been left unattended for more than a couple of minutes. Some of us were a bit sceptical about the extent of his disability but he had a medical card which he would wave around when challenged to prove his case. Incidentally, the challenge was usually issued by the unfortunate customer who had just nipped to the toilet only to return to find a wee jakey-looking guy trying to make off with his booze.

I got on the chat with one of the guys in *Monty's* and remarked that his accent didn't sound entirely local. It seems that the bloke was originally from Alaska and he had landed up in Inverness as a merchant seaman. That was about 20 years ago and he liked it so much he just stayed. You really have to wonder what the hell Alaska is like if he thinks *Monty's* is a model of sophistication.

John's comments: Craig may be right about Gellions *being the oldest pub in Inverness by date, but one of the locals I was talking to mentioned a pub called* The Market Bar.

Now I have a vague memory that a year or two ago we visited this pub, which if my memory is right, was a real man's pub which I think may have some interesting oldest claims, other than date. So it was my choice as the next pub to visit.

John's 1st Pub: *The Market Bar;* We wandered out of *Gellions*, and, following instructions from the barman Monty, got lost. Following more instructions from a friendly local, we went up another wee lane off Academy Street and into *The Market*.

What a pub this is. *Gellions* may have a claim to be included in this book. It is seemingly the oldest in date order, but my *Market Bar* has four claims to be in the book: it must have the oldest furniture, decor, toilets, and certainly the oldest and most decrepit locals in Inverness. It's a brilliant bar.

The barmaid Melonie had her hands full keeping the crazy locals in order. I doubt if any tourists come in. Even if they did find it they would get a hell of a shock when they got in. Mind you, if, like me, they came from Govan, they would feel quite at home.

One of the worthies at the bar who was adamant about not revealing his name, (I think he wanted to sound interesting) said that if we mentioned him in the book there would be trouble, so Harry, your secret is safe with me.

Melonie has her hands full controlling the locals

It may not be the oldest by date, but is definitely worth a visit to see what the mature locals spend their time doing, and is that not what travel is all about!

We had a great time and even Craig had to admit that it was an interesting pick. He was none to happy with the state of the toilets. As you know, he's a bit of a cleanliness freak. He attempts to leave every toilet he visits without touching the door handles. Sometimes he can be a while.

Craig's comments: This pub was exactly as I remembered it, and believe me I had been trying hard to forget it. Only kidding! Yes, The Market is a bit of a dump, but sometimes that's the way we like our boozers.

I have no idea how old the pub is but one of the customers showed me some damage to a section of the outside wall. He claimed it had happened when it had been used to sharpen the bayonets of government troops before the battle of Culloden in 1746. Apparently some of the troops had been billeted in The Market.

Craig's 2nd Pub: My next pub was the *Phoenix Ale House* and fortunately it was just across the road from *Blackfriars*. The good fortune comes, not just from the proximity of the two pubs, but the fact that the bus station is a mere five minute walk away. Being close to the bus station is always a consideration when finishing a day out sampling beer in a far-off town.

We had been to T*he Phoenix* on a previous visit to Inverness and had found it to be a nice tidy wee pub. I say we, but to be honest my travelling companion had no real memory of ever being in the place. John often slags me off for hoarding things but sometimes he has to admit that it can come in handy.

When I told him that we would be revisiting the pub he said he couldn't remember being in it. I didn't have a copy of our book handy to show him the evidence of our past visit but I did have my camera. On the memory chip of the camera I still have every picture I've ever taken on our various trips around Scotland. Scrolling back through the years of pictures I eventually found the photo I was looking for. It is not a picture which actually appeared in the book as it was a bit too X certificate for publication. The

59

photo was taken at the end of a very long, beer-fuelled day and John wasn't looking at his best. In normal circumstances it would have been a useful piece of blackmail material, but since John cannot be embarrassed I could only use it to annoy him.

As soon as we entered the pub I realised that I too had forgotten some of the features of the place. I noticed that the island bar had a small gutter running all the way round it. Technically it should be referred to as a Terrazzo Spittoon.

Coming from a mining community, where many men were in the habit of chewing tobacco, I could see the usefulness of such a feature.

Our barman, Danny, assured me that it was more or less decorative nowadays, with only the odd befuddled numpty using it for its original purpose.

He told us although the pub is quite old it was originally built as a girls' school. It dates from 1841and apparently it was converted into a pub in the 1890s.

George and Danny run a 'Flaming' good pub

This was quite disappointing as it ruled out *The Phoenix* from being close to the oldest pub in Inverness. But, as ever, we soldiered on with sampling the quality of the beer.

By that time we had been joined by John's brother, Robert, who proved himself worthy of the Mackay name by enthusiastically wiring into the booze.

While we were enjoying our second, or possibly third, pint the owner, George MacLean came in and Danny introduced him to us. George has another great bar in Inverness, *The Castle*.

There has been a lot of money spent doing up *The Phoenix* and George has a lot of plans for upgrading the food and entertainment. There was a good selection of beers with at least seven fonts dispensing real ale. Apparently real ale has become very popular in recent years especially among younger drinkers and other such posers.

Although George only bought *The Phoenix* in 2014 he has completely turned it around. On our last visit the pub was really shabby and dark. Not to mention empty. All that has changed and the pub has now become one of the most popular watering holes in the city.

It was therefore a bit of a shock to find out that the pub was put back on the market in March of 2015. It would seem that George has decided to take things a bit easier after 50 years in the business.

John's comment's: Craig's second bar was nice enough, and you could take the wife there without fear of abuse. But for me the atmosphere was too clean and the place was too nice to be a real old bar. But it is worth visiting if you're in town.

John's 2nd Pub: *Blackfriar's*; We had come this far so we had to finish off the day by visiting the final bar we had heard mentioned.

Big John gets lumbered with wee John in Blackfriars

This is a big bar and it was made to look bigger by the fact that when we went in there was only one customer, Big John, who, when we introduced ourselves, told us he was a bus driver, so we had a lot in common. God knows what size the driver's cabins are like up north; he looked like a lumberjack, and a big one at that.

Dell and Janette Graeme run the place and filled us in on its history. Although the building went up in 1793, it was not used as a pub. Its name when it first served alcohol was, *Fraser's Temperance Hotel* and that was in 1867, so *The Gellions* is still the oldest.

Blackfriars is about the seventh name it has had, mind you. That is in a period of about 200 years, so it has had an interesting past. More interesting to us was what the bar was like today, and it was very good, with a great selection of bevy and live music.

Dell and Janette

Inverness is blessed with a lot of great bars and today we visited four of the oldest. They were all good in different ways, but all the bars had live music. I think there are more musicians and singers in Inverness than anywhere else we have visited. Inverness should be renamed 'Scotland's Highland Fling Capital'.

Craig's comments: *I've lost count of the number of times I've been in Blackfriars. That might suggest that I quite like the place. It should, because I do. Still don't know how old it is.*

John: It had been a great day in Inverness and the fact that we had been joined by my brother Robert and his partner Ruth for the last couple of hours made it even better.

Just as the Gold Bus left, the driver announced that there would be no hospitality service until we reached Perth, Craig was away again, his moaning travelling South was just as bad as it was on the journey North.

Find oor Auld Boozers

by Bus . . . .

The Gold Bus from Buchanan Street Bus Station, non-stop, right into Inverness Bus Station.

. . . . then by Boot

'Gellions' (and 'Monty's)

Gellions', and *'Monty's'* are on High Street which runs down to the river at the end of Academy Street. 'Monty's is up a wee lane beside and behind *'Gellions'*.

'Pheonix' and 'Blackfriars'

The Phoenix' and 'Blackfriars' are on Academy Street which is just down the street that takes you out of the Bus Station.

'The Market'

'The Market Bar' is hidden away (and so it should be) in a wee lane off Academy Street.

Glasgow (the right side)

John: Scotland's biggest, and most people would say best, city in Scotland. These people are called Glaswegians, and they may, or may not, be right.

But are the oldest pubs in Glasgow the best, or even the oldest, in Scotland? Our task was in front of us. And we never shirk from tasks, or pubs. So off we went.

The first thing our research told us was something we already knew. There were too many pubs in Glasgow to cover in one chapter. What would we do?

I think it may have been Craig, or maybe me, who came up with the idea of splitting Glasgow in two and having a couple of chapters. When you think that Glasgow and its outskirts house a huge percentage of the population of Scotland, we knew it was worth at least two chapters. So two it was.

You will see from the map above that we have split the city from top to bottom, right through George Square. If you can imagine the line going right down Queen Street, and carrying on downward, and upward, that is where the split is.

We thought about using the Clyde as the split, but most of the pubs, at least the well-known ones, would be in the north of the city.

Mind you, I don't know if I'm happy with that statement, as places like my beloved Govan, not to mention the Gorbals, Govanhill and other great pub places have old pubs that are a must to visit, but then again, these areas might not be the most politically beautiful areas- but they are my favourites, so there! By the way, is there such a statement as 'politically beautiful'. I think I made it up, but never mind.

So the two of us did a bit of research, by that I mean that Craig would find one pub and we would take it from there!

As you can imagine, even for us, visiting the pubs in Glasgow that claim to be the oldest is not a one day visit. Our job's a nightmare. I wish the wives agreed.

We decided to start with the right hand side of the city. So this chapter is everything to the right of George Square.

As always, I have given Craig the first chance to pick a pub he thinks is the oldest.

Craigs 1st Pub: *The Old College Bar:* This pub was my choice as a contender for the title of Glasgow's oldest pub. One look at the building would be enough to get it a nomination at least. It sits about half way up High Street just up and across from High Street railway station.

That station sits on the site of the old university from which it takes its name. The university stood on that site from 1460 until 1870 and, like most universities, ale houses saw a lot of trade from its student body and staff. To my untrained eye *the Old College Bar* certainly looks as if it was around when the first students arrived to take up their studies. In other words it looks about ready to fall down of its own accord. This will not happen of course as the bar is soon to be demolished.

Old codgers gather outside The Old College

In a recent newspaper interview the owner admitted that he had applied for permission to demolish the pub with a view to building a 'new *Old College Bar*' at some time in the future. Personally I think that this is unlikely ever to happen. Once a pub closes it tends to stay that way. Besides how the hell can you have a new old pub?

We have visited many, many pubs on our little adventures and quite a few of those pubs have totally unexpected interiors. That is to say the outside and the inside don't match. With *the Old College Bar* there is no such conflict. What you see outside is pretty much what you get inside, old and clapped out. Don't get me wrong I really liked the pub. It's the kind of pub I grew up with. It is just a bit unnerving to walk in off the street and step back into the early 1970s, although the prices have unfortunately been updated.

I would describe the interior lighting as subdued, possibly to give a calm atmosphere for the customers but more likely because the dodgy wiring has given up the ghost. While I'm on the subject of ghosts it would seem that, like every other pub more than 30 years old, *The Old College* has its very own ghost. As ever, the spirit in question does most of its haunting down in the cellar. Apparently part of the old cobblestone High Street is still visible down there. The select band of people who have the ability to see the ghost insist that the spectre takes the form of an old university professor. Legend has it that the old boy keeps returning to the bar to pay his outstanding bar tab.

Apart from not believing in ghosts, I find it hard to believe that paying an outstanding bar bill would be enough to draw anyone or anything back from the great beyond on a regular basis. If there was anything to the story I would think it was far more likely that the ancient teacher had been short changed at some time and refused to rest in peace until he got his cash back.

Historically the pub was used by staff and students of the University. The students were allowed to drink on the ground floor of the pub, while the tutors sat upstairs, presumably in more luxurious surroundings. Obviously that was a long time ago as any hint of luxury has long since left the building.

On the day of our visit the pub was fairly busy. In fact we got the last space at the bar. Almost straightaway we got into conversation with one of the customers.

John Hainning is a regular and told us all about the ongoing problem of the pub's imminent demolition. He told us that it has been threatened with closure for years now, but no date for this has ever been finalised. There has, of course, been a petition doing the rounds trying to save the place but, as ever, I think it will all come down to money. Despite the dilapidated condition of the building the little pub still makes a profit.

Our barman, Grant McMurtry, joined in on the conversation, but point-blank refused to have his picture taken. I did think about asking if he was just a bit shy, on a witness protection scheme or just keeping a low profile with a view to staying out of police custody. But since he was bigger younger and stronger than me I decided that shyness was probably the answer and silence was my best option.

The twa Johns

We asked both Grant and John if they had any amusing pub related tales to tell us. Between them they told us a short story about a well-known professional photographer. He had decided to use the Old College Bar as a backdrop to a photo shoot he was planning. He turned up one day with a model in tow. The model turned out to be of the scantily clad variety.

As I have said, *the College* is a nice comfortable place to have a wee drink, and the photographer certainly thought so as well as he proceeded to make full use of the gantry. By the time he got going with his camera he was well plastered. After only a few minutes snapping away on the waste ground at the back of the pub, gravity got the better of him and he keeled over. Unable to get back up, some of the pub customers and the bikini clad model had to carry him back into the pub, presumably for a couple of medicinal whiskies. There is no record of the photo shoot appearing in any publications.

The Old College has regular entertainment, and these events are well attended. Among other customers we talked was an older man. He told us that he had appeared on TV and films. I spent a good five minutes trying to remember which programmes I'd seen him in before he put me out of my misery and told me that he was an extra and not actually a romantic lead.

Another old boy I met went by the name of Peter the Singer and he too refuse to pose for my camera. By this time I was convinced that this pub must be a refuge for people with identity issues, possibly mob related. Anyway old Peter was a great fan of Junior football so we had a good chat about the differing levels of ability shown by Ayrshire and Glasgow teams. I had a copy of our last book with me so I felt able to hold my own in the discussion. To be honest it was more of a trip down memory lane than a discussion. Everyone we spoke to was saying that *The Old College* was indeed the oldest pub in Glasgow and I have to say that just looking at the place, it was hard to argue. According to Grant the rear part of the building had become dangerously unstable and had been demolished a few years back.

When we left the pub we nipped round the back to see what kind of a job they had made of it. Looking at the results all I can say is the remaining building seems to be held up by not much more than faith alone. Obviously I'm no structural engineer, but I would guess that if several really heavy pigeons land on the back corner of the roof, all at the same time, there will be no need for the bulldozers.

We were just about to make our way back down High Street when I noticed something which shook my idea that *The Old College* was the oldest pub in Glasgow. The sign, right above the front door, proclaims that the pub has been in business since 1810.

I was devastated, somehow I had got it into my head that the original pub had opened its doors at about the same time as the university. Luckily John had been hitting the booze like someone who had just heard that prohibition was about to be introduced, so I don't think he noticed the sign. I wasn't about to point it out to him.

What I can't understand is why nobody bothered to tell us what age the pub really was. Then again, given the fact that we were investigating the oldest pubs in the toon, maybe we should have thought to ask.

John's comments: *Craig had told me he wanted to visit the* Old College Bar *as soon as possible as the building and the ones surrounding it are going to be demolished, or so the plan is, but I wouldn't be surprised if it's still there now.*

If it is, give it a try as it is a real old fashioned pub with a great atmosphere and some interesting old locals.

Having said that, the area around the pub would be greatly improved if they did pull the whole lot down.

Johns 1st Pub: *The Press Bar.* This bar was not even on the radar as one I might pick as my first choice. I planned to listen to locals in Craig's first pub and take it from there. However, on our walk to *The Old College Bar,* we were talking about pubs we had visited when we were young, and lo and behold, we found ourselves outside *The Press Bar.* What else could we do but nick in for a quick one. Nostalgia is a better reason than most of the ones we use for going into a pub. Craig used to drink there at lunch time when he was at a local university, and having served my time as a compositor, I had visited the place a few times when I was young. Years ago it was always full of newspaper people having a quick one while still on the clock. The reason I went there was to try and meet someone who would get me a job in one of the newspapers. The wages in the papers were about double what someone in the real printing trade got.

We were surprised when we saw the pub, as we both thought it had been pulled down years ago.

The reason this pub is featured in the book is that, while I was talking to the present owner Vince McEntee, I mentioned to him the reason for our visit to Glasgow today. He told me that since 1928, 'The Press Bar' has been owned and managed by the same family, longer than any pub in Glasgow. That is quite an achievement, and as far as I'm concerned makes it a shoo-in for an entry in this book.

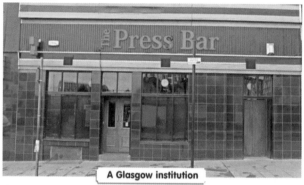
A Glasgow institution

When we went in at first and told Vince what we were doing, I think he thought we were a couple of old chancers, and he's right, but when we showed him a previous book and explained ourselves more clearly to him, he warmed to us and in no time at all he was almost smiling.

The barmaid, Lindsay Docherty, was a good laugh. And what a busy girl she is. When I asked her if she had worked for long in the pub, she told me she had been working here part time for only a few months. She is at University, has a five year old kid and still has time to teach Irish Dancing. If she had used the Irish Dancing pose she teaches, she probably wouldn't have had the kid! Only kidding Lindsay.

This is a great man's pub, one of the best I have visited. There is a rectangular bar in the middle of the pub and the walls have great old pictures. Another brilliant thing is that there is only one telly, which was showing the horses with the sound down. That's how it should be in a man's pub. There was also no sign of food or weans. A bar that ticks all the boxes.

I knew that in the old days the place was used by the reporters and printers who worked, or let's just say produced newspapers, and I wanted to find out if any really famous people had visited the bar. Vince told me that hundreds of famous people had visited the bar, too many to mention, but he did whip out a photograph with the Hollywood star Christopher Walken (star of the Deer Hunter and many more epics). He was brought in by the equally famous star photographer of the day, Harry Benson. I was really impressed.

Vince, Lindsay and Stuart

There was one really loud customer at the end of the bar. When I say loud, it was not his voice, but his jumper that was loud. The blokes name was Stuart Urie, and he works for a company that sells, among other things, Christmas Jumpers. The problem for Stuart is that he feels obliged to show off the merchandise. His attempt a selling us one fell on deaf ears. Craig and I look ridiculous enough without wearing loud jumpers. Apart from his jumper, he was a really nice bloke, as were all the customers who all joined in the patter. We had a really great time in the *The Press Bar*.

If you're in Glasgow with the wife, this is a great haven in which to spend a couple of hours while she wanders around 'The Merchant City' or some other crazy shopping area in the city saving you a fortune on everything she buys.

Talking about 'Irish Dancing', reminds me of a story of a wee Glasgow bloke who was dragged by the wife to see 'Riverdance', or some show like that. The problem was that being small, with big people sitting in front of him, he could only see the dancers from the waist up. He thought the show was crap. You can imagine it, can't you!

Craig's comments: Only John could include a pub that is only fractionally older than himself in a book about historical hostelries. I think his decision to include The Press Bar had more to do with a dry throat than a thirst for knowledge.

It is a good bar and almost exactly as it was the last time I saw it, twenty years ago.

The Press Bar might not have a great deal of history behind it, but it is well worth a visit. If you can find it.

Craigs 2nd Bar: I chose *The Scotia* as one of my contenders for the title 'The Auldest Boozer in Toon' for two simple reasons. The first reason is that it looks really old. The second, and slightly more convincing, reason for making it onto my list was the fact that the pub claims to be the oldest on its web site. That's enough of a reason for me.

Although I can never claim to have been a regular in The Scotia, I was a frequent visitor for about five years back in the 1990s.

It's a real man's pub: nae carpets and nae weans, perfect! It does attract a fairly large female clientele at certain times of the week. The Scotia is a great music pub with live bands playing four nights out of seven. Almost every genre of music can be heard in the pub, everything from traditional folk to heavy rock.

I have spent many a great night in there listening to some of Scotland's most talented musicians. Possibly the best I ever heard there was the late, great Michael Marra. Apparently Billy Connolly was one of the most famous entertainers to appear in the pub, often alongside Gerry Rafferty.

The Scotia's association with music actually has quite a long history. Back in 1862 the imaginatively titled Scotia Music Hall was built right next door to the pub.

John has also visited *The Scotia* before, but he doesn't know it as well as I do. For instance, I happen to know that not only is there a writers group associated with the pub, but there is also a poetry club who hold their regular meetings in there.

The Scotia Bar, Glasgow

This was information I was desperate to keep from him, as I have been on the receiving end of some of his attempts at poetry before. He definitely leans more towards William McGonigall than Robert Burns. There was no way I could let him sign up for a group session. I had to think of the impact on our book sales.

After a quick thirst-quenching drink (you never really taste the first one) we got on the chart with the barmaid Joanna. She was really good company even if she did let the cat out the bag about the poetry thing.

It seems that *The Scotia* is bucking the trend as far as declining numbers of customers is concerned. Over the last few years, on our ongoing investigation into Scottish boozers, we have seen a marked reduction in the numbers of dedicated pint swillers attending their local pubs.

When we asked Joanna and Allan, the bar staff, if they had any humorous tales to tell us about life behind the bar, Allan said that apart from the time a horse wandered into the pub he couldn't recollect anything too outrageous.

Before we could quiz him about the incident he had to leave to serve another punter. While we are waiting for his return I decided to fill the gap by telling a story of my own.

A while back I was having a quiet beer in *The Scotia*- actually it was too quiet and I decided to move over the road to the *Clutha Bar*. The barman had told me that there was a band playing over there later that day.

Before I could make the move a wee, and obviously drunk, man came staggering in, and was immediately flung back out again by the barman.

Twenty minutes later, while I was sitting on a bar stool in *The Clutha* sipping my beer, the same wee man came staggering in. He ordered a hauf 'n' a hauf pint and immediately started telling all us customers what a bad-tempered bastard the barman over the road was.

Joanna and Allan

If he hadn't been quite so drunk his day would have gone much more smoothly. Firstly, he wouldn't have been chucked out of *The Scotia.* Secondly, he would have realised that the bad-tempered barman from *The Scotia* had finished his shift over there and was now standing behind the bar in *The Clutha.*

Apparently his mood had not improved very much. I base this assumption on the fact that the wee man was quickly launched through the doors of his second pub of the day.

The Scotia first opened its doors in 1792. To put that into historical context, when the first pints were being pulled in the bar the French were not long started with their revolution. You could say that while the barmaids were putting heads on pints the French were putting heads in baskets.

The bar has three sections to it. There is a small snug at one end, then the main bar and finally what might be called the entertainment section. This is where the bands and the folk singers set up to play. There is a CCTV installed so that the acts can be seen through in the main bar.

A major feature of the pub is the low-beamed ceiling, which in the bad old days, when smoking was allowed in bars, created a bit of an atmosphere. One you could cut with a knife.

Nowadays, the place is spotless and well maintained. We found the staff to be efficient and happy to chat to their customers.

The Scotia is one of Glasgow's most famous pubs and its position, close to the city centre, means that it attracts a healthy chunk of the tourist trade.

Personally, I have always used the pub as a meeting place when getting together with friends before setting out on one of our occasional pub crawls.

For a pub so close to the city centre the prices are very reasonable. In fact the only person I've ever heard complaining about the cost of a round was John. For once we were not working with a kitty and he was forced to dig into his own pocket to pay for his drink. He even had the cheek to query the cost with Joanna.

Quick as a flash she replied, 'I said we were the oldest pub in Glasgow, I didn't say we were the cheapest'.

On the face of it *The Scotia* has a good claim to being Glasgow's oldest pub but, as I soon discovered, there was a problem. And it was a problem which could give John the upper hand in our competition to find the auldest boozer in Glesga toon.

There is no doubt that the pub first opened its doors to the drinking public in 1792 That fact alone should assure it of the title but it seems that the pub hasn't kept those doors open continuously since that time.

Apparently *The Scotia* ceased trading in 1906 and didn't re-open for almost a quarter of a century. When it did open again it had been remodelled into the pub we see today, more or less.

I might have been able to overlook this if it had only been closed once. There is a good chance John would never find out about the pub being closed way back then, but unfortunately the pub was also shut in the early 1970s.

One of the barmen told us that a biker gang called 'The Blue Angels' used to drink in the pub and caused a lot of bother in the local area. Eventually the authorities decided that shutting The Scotia down was the only way of stopping the trouble. The pub didn't open again until 1987.

Presumably, in the intervening years, a combination of alcohol abuse, powerful motorbikes and the odd 'rumble' has thinned out the ranks of The Blue Angels. Whatever the reason they don't seem to be on the scene anymore.

Given that the pub is now full of would-be writers and poets I don't suppose any self-respecting Blue Angel would want to be seen in the place.

My problem with claiming that *The Scotia* is the oldest pub in Glasgow is the amount of time the pub was actually shut. Can you claim that it was still a pub when it was lying empty for so many years? To my mind, if a pub is not selling any booze for such a considerable time it is not really a pub any more. A downright crime perhaps, but not a pub!

Therefore, much as I would like to claim that my first choice of pub was indeed the oldest one in Glasgow I have to admit defeat. I realise that this will no doubt result in John taking the piss, now and forever more.

John's comments; I thought that it would be difficult to criticize Craig's choice of The Scotia Bar. *Its web page and most of the locals seem to confirm it as the oldest pub!*

However, and this is a big however, I was talking to an old timer, I think his name was Ivor, and he told me that he had been told that during the early 1900s The Scotia *had been closed for about 20 years before opening again. Even more astonishing, he then said that the same had happened in the 1970s into the 80s.*

It could end up that The Scotia *is the oldest pub in Glasgow that's been shut twice. It's still a claim, of sorts.*

With this sensational information tucked away in the back of my mind, I asked the barmaid, Joanna, if she knew of any other really old pubs in the city.

She told me that she knew of a pub out east (near the Barras) called Hielan Jessie *which claims to be an old bar, but more importantly to me, if not Craig, was the fact that she said that it was a great old traditional bar. She told me in a whisper so nobody in the bar would hear her talking about another bar in Glasgow worth a visit. Mind you, it was the same whispered voice that told me about the day, many years ago, when a horse came in to* The Scotia*! I'm going to tell Craig that it's my next choice,* Hielan Jessie's *that is, not the Horse.*

John's 2ⁿᵈ Pub; *Hielan Jessie;* Craig said this bar would suit me as I was a big Jessie. I ignored him. I said that this is my choice, so we're going. I also mentioned that as far as I knew, it didn't shut for a few years every now and then. This annoyed him.

The pub is on the Gallowgate, near the Barras, so it is easy to find. It was just a pity our visit didn't coincide with the Barras being open so I could indulge in my favourite lump of grease, 'Danny's Do-Nuts'. Yes, that's how they spell it.

As soon as we went in the door, I knew I would like this pub. It's a real man's bar. The first thing I noticed was that there was not even one TV. I think this is the first pub I can remember that is tellyless. If anyone reading this knows of another, let me know.

The owner, Billy Gould, and the barmaid, May Milliken, were great company. When I mentioned the no tellies, he told me that if any strangers come in wanting to watch a match that is being shown on telly, he or May make sure they have ordered a drink before they find out there's none.

Hielan Jessie, Glasgow

Although this is a brilliant bar and the walls are filled with interesting memorabilia, I first of all had to try and find out if the pub should be in the running for the oldest pub in Glasgow. The building that houses the pub has a sign saying it was built in 1771, which would make it one of the oldest. Billy was honest enough to admit that although he has owned the pub for 28 years, and his father before him, the oldest he can trace the pub is back to is 1826, when it was called *The Regal*. He had a photograph of the pub, and it was a real old photo, so the information is accurate.

I believe this puts *Hielan Jessie* in line for the title of the oldest pub in Glasgow, I think. Talking about long serving people, May told me that she had worked in '*The Jessie*' for 28 years. I think child labour must have been allowed in these days as, when she introduced herself, I thought she was Billy's daughter. Billy was none too chuffed.

To change the subject, I asked him how the pub got its name. It is a great story. Long ago, when Britain had an empire,

80

there was the famous Indian Mutiny in 1857. Jessie was married to one of the soldiers of the 78th Highland regiment, who were under siege at the time, and things were looking bleak. Just as it looked as if the end was close, Jessie heard the sound of the pipes in the distance and rallied the troops, who fought on heroically until the relief troops arrived. She was the hero of the day and is well remembered in the history of the 78th Highlanders.

Billy makes his feelings known about the authors

Getting back to today, the pub was busy, even though it was early doors on a cold Monday morning. Most of the regulars looked as if they might have fought in the uprising, but I though better than to ask. They are a tough looking lot, but brilliant company.

One of the regulars, Kenny Taylor, has a great claim to fame. He was the first player in Scotland to score a hat trick of goals not from open play. He was playing for Ashfield Juniors when he scored the goals, two were direct from corners and the other was a free kick. So this is another reason this pub should be in the book. It's the pub with the oldest regular who scored three goals not from open play. They should put that sign outside the door. Kenny and the rest of the regulars were great company.

One of the walls in the pub is completely covered in black and white photographs, all of them of ladies. There were no men

81

that I could see, and the photographs looked very professional. I asked Billy what was the story behind them. Seemingly, they were all taken by the famous Italian painter Horatio McCulloch. At one time, Horatio had six paintings on display in the Kelvingrove Art Gallery, so he was some artist. It's a funny name for an Italian. All I could find out was that he was born in 1805, the same year as the battle of Trafalgar, so it is believed he was named after Horatio Nelson, the hero of the hour. By this time I had had a few and forgot to ask the question I had meant to ask to start with. That was how he came to have the second name McCulloch. I still don't know.

A more interesting story about Horatio was that he had a wee white Scottie dog which he brought in with him when he was having an espresso or a pint of heavy more likely. Anyway Horatio has long gone to the art gallery in the sky, but the ghost of his wee white Scottie dog has been seen in the ladies toilet on several occasions. Now, I have no doubt the story is true, but I couldn't help wondering where the wee dog was before ladies toilets were installed in pubs. I think it was well after Horatio's time.

Billy and May

During my chat with the locals, Craig had been talking to May, but he was none too chuffed when Billy placed a Bar Runner on the bar in front of him with the words 'Bullshit Corner' emblazoned on it. Billy said there was a good reason for it being placed there. Craig made no comment!

Another good thing about the 'Jessie' is that the regulars raise lots of money for good causes. The night before our visit, one of the local girls had shaved her head to help raise money for her sister, who has cancer. I hope she has recovered and wish her all the best.

We had spent a long time in *The Jessie* and enjoyed every minute. This is one of the best pubs we have ever visited and a must if you are in the area. For all I know, it may even be the oldest pub in Glasgow.

Craig's comments: Absolutely no complaints about Heilan Jessie's; *it is a great pub. I just wish that I had heard of it years ago. I would say that it is really what is missing from the pub that makes it a new favourite of mine: no telly, no carpets and no weans. Ideal!*

Unfortunately, for John, it is not as old as he claimed it was. Although the date, 1792, is carved into the outside wall of the pub, the pub itself has not been located there for all that time. The origin of the pub's name should really have alerted us to its real age, but we were otherwise occupied on the day of our visit.

Legend has it that the pub was named in honour of Jessie, heroine of the siege of 1857. That siege was part of the Indian Mutiny which, as every schoolboy, but very few drunks will know, took place in 1857. It does not take much of a detective to work out that the pub couldn't have been in existence before that time.

In fact, pubs bearing the 'Jessie's' name have been in two other locations before ending up in this area of the Gallowgate.

All I can say to John, as far as finding Glasgow's oldest pub, is keep looking.

John: Well, that's the right hand side of Glasgow covered, I hope the pubs we visit in the left hand side of the city will be just as good, and just as old. Time will tell.

Find oor Auld Boozers

by Bus . . . .

If you don't know how to get to Glasgow, you're aff your heid.

. . . . then by Boot

Old College Bar

'*Old College Bar*', it's about a five minute walk up High Street from Glasgow Cross. It's on the left opposite High Street Railway Station.

The Press Bar

'*The Press Bar*' is in Albion Street. From George Square area, just walk along Ingram Street and take a left into Albion Street. The pub's on your left in the Herald Building.

The Scotia Bar

'*The Scotia*', Walk along Argyle Street, going away from the Central Station. At Mark and Spencers, turn right and go a couple of hundred yards down Stockwell Street. It's on your right.

Hielan Jessie

'**Hielan Jessie**', Head for the Barras and get onto the Gallogate, you'll find it no bother.

Glasgow (the left side)

John: To the left hand side of George Square. Some will say the more glamorous side of the city. Some will say no. I'll leave it up to you. Having said that, it's not glamour we're after. In fact, you could say the very opposite. Remember, it's pubs, and old ones, we're trying to find. Usually they are not the most glamorous in the city, well not in Glasgow. Or am I wrong? I usually am.

Like the right, there are thousands of pubs in the left hand side of George Square. We were on a hiding to nothing. No matter what we come up with as the oldest pub will not be the one most of our readers think.

As is our tradition, Craig had the first pick of an old pub, so here we go with the left hand side of Glasgow.

Craig's 1st Pub: *Sloan's,* in the Argyle Arcade would not be my first or even second choice of pub to visit on a day out in Glasgow. In fact it would be pretty near the bottom of a very long list of pubs worth spending any time in. But John had put his foot down insisting we needed to visit it to balance up his grand plan of checking out old pubs to the east and west of George Square.

One obvious flaw in his little scheme is the fact that Sloan's is not really a pub. Well, not in the accepted sense of that term, and since I was the one who had to write about the place I was going to be the one setting the terms. Let's face it what kind of pub has a grand ballroom?

To their credit the owners of Sloan's do not claim that the bar is even close to being the oldest pub in Glasgow. They do claim however that Sloan's is the oldest bar/ restaurant in Glasgow. That, I expect, is why John wanted to us to visit the place. He doesn't need much of an excuse at the best of times.

The building which now houses Sloan's bars, bistro restaurant and ballroom started out as a coffee house back in the late 18th century. It was only in the early 20th century that it was developed into what it is today.

Architecturally the Grade A listed building is a real gem. Everywhere you look there are exotic woods used in the decoration. The great mahogany staircase leading to the other two floors of the building is a feature worth taking a look at.

If you enter the pub through the Argyle Arcade entrance the staircase can be seen at its best. Going in that way will also give

86

you an idea of what you can expect when it comes to paying for your drink. There are more than 30 jewellery and diamond shops lining the arcade, although they probably don't refer to them as mere shops.

I have been in this bar a few times but for one very good reason these visits have always been kept rather short. The price of booze is enough to drive you to drink somewhere else.

Argyle Street entrance to Sloans

When he had to pay for our round John went uncharacteristically quiet and the colour drained from his face. I thought he was going to keel over. Fortunately, for John, that didn't happen, as there was no way I was going to catch him.

For the same order we had been charged two pounds more than we had paid at *Heilan Jessie's*, only a half mile up the road.

To make matters worse they didn't even have Tennent's Lager on draught. That was pretty hard to take given that the Brewery is only about a mile away. I suspect a bit of snobbery is going on here.

Just to underline how far out of our comfort zone we really were, I spied baby changing facilities in the gents toilet. I know we could be accused of being a wee bit old school, but when did things start going this crazy?

I`m happy to say that the bar staff we met more than made up for any of the annoying aspects of this bar. Both were from well outside Glasgow. One was from Lewis and the other came from Lithuania. Both incomers to the city, and it was really amusing to listen to John trying to work out where they came from.

In his defence it can be quite hard to differentiate between a Lewis accent and a Lithuanian one. Actually, even when he did manage to get who was who, he was well past the stage of being able to pronounce Lithuanian. Eventually he settled for referring to the bloke as Russian.

We couldn't afford to stay in Sloan's for the rest of the afternoon as John`s blood pressure was unlikely to take the strain of parting with such large amounts of cash. We settled for one last round, which I paid for while he was in the toilet. No sense risking a medical emergency.

John's comments: Sloans *advertises itself as Glasgow's oldest Bar/Restaurant, so it's not really a stand-alone bar. I wasn't worried as it is old and sells drink. Although it was Craig's first pick, he is not that enamoured with the place because the bar doubles as a restaurant, and if you are in at lunch time, especially at the weekend, all you can smell is food. It is good food, mind you, but it is not my idea of a traditional pub. But is it Glasgow's oldest? I'm not sure.*

John's 1st Pub: *The Three Judges;* A few weeks ago while we were visiting *Hielan Jessies*, I asked the owner, Allan, if he knew of any old pubs in the left hand side of the city. He was not sure, but suggested that I visit *The Three Judges*, and ask the bar manager Angela Bradley, who is a friend of his, if she had any ideas of oldies in the Partick/West End area of the city. So on a bright but cold Monday morning in February, we wandered into *The Three Judges*.

My first impression was that it was a nice looking pub with a fair amount of regulars for a Monday morning. We introduced ourselves to the bar manager, who was indeed Angela. When she understood the reason for our visit she did her best to come up with a really old pub in the area, or one which was older than '*TTJ*'. There were none that she knew of that had a big claim to be really old. One of the regulars told us that *Curlers*, up on Byres Road was pretty old, but recently had been turned into a modern 'Retro' type bar. I pretended I knew what this meant, but it didn't sound good. However, since it may be old, Craig said he would take it on as his next bar if we used '*TTJ*' as an oldie.

It's a pints decision at The Three Judges

The bar had some really old and interesting memorabilia on the walls and ceiling, but I would have to find some real old reason to feature this pub in our book.

It was then that I started talking to a regular at the bar. Frank was his name, and he told me a frankly great story about the history of the bar, which led to its inclusion.

I had thought that the name *The Three Judges* was something to do with the legal profession. But no, this pub is the oldest boxing pub in Glasgow. 'Tell me more' I begged Frank. He first of all pointed high up on the wall at the end of the bar, and there were mounted the three cards the boxing judges used during the fights to show who they thought had won each round. At each end of the cards were mounted two bells, the ones that sounded at the start and end of each round. Not only that, but he asked Angela to show us the pair of original gloves that were used in a bout. As I held the gloves, I thought I felt their power surging through me. I was about to give Craig a good right hook, but managed to hold myself in check. Maybe the drink was taking effect, who knows! This was great. Here I was standing in a piece of real Glasgow History. I was full of emulsion.

Angela is a real knockout

Angela said that the pub had moved away from the boxing theme as a bad crowd was becoming the norm in the pub, and fights were common that had nothing to do with the noble art.

Another interesting piece of memorabilia are the thousands of Pump Font Clips that are mounted on the ceiling behind the bar. Over the years, some 20,000 have been collected. I found this hard to believe, as this means 20,000 different beers. No wonder we drink.

Not only is this pub a shoo in for this book, but it is the type of pub that we like. Good beer and a great barmaid as well as

90

friendly regulars. No carpets or kids, and the only food they sell is Pork Pies for £1.50. There was one telly, but it was off, so that was good as well.

An additional important piece of information I discovered is that most of the regulars lean towards 'The Partick Thistle', 'The Harry Wrags', 'The Maryhill Magyars', Glasgow's greatest team. Did I mention I was once a ball-boy at Firhill!

I was well chuffed with my first pub in the left hand side of Glasgow. I doubt if Craig will be as happy with his next, 'Retro' pub, but you never know.

Craig's comments: I very much doubt that just having a vague notion has ever worked out particularly well when choosing a winner. Just ask one of those blokes who hang about outside their local 'turf accountants'. But it does describe John's reasoning when choosing The Three Judges *as a contender for Glasgow's oldest pub. I'm fairly sure that in the whole time we were in the place no one ever mentioned the age of the pub. Not that it really mattered since I had already found the oldest one.*

That being said The Three Judges *was a great wee pub. It is a traditionally decorated high ceilinged bar with plenty of seating and a stage area. The beer was good and the patter was even better. If we had been looking for a contender for best local pub this place would be in with a shout. However since we were looking for the oldest boozer it was obvious to me that John was on to yet another loser.*

Craig's 2nd Pub: *The Curlers Rest;* While we were in *The Three Judges* a couple of people had mentioned that a bar just a short walk up Byres Road was thought to be the oldest pub in the area. *The Curlers Rest* didn't sound like a traditional name for a good Scottish pub. My first impression was that this name would be better suited to an upmarket hairdressers. As the day went on I became convinced that my first impression was correct.

Someone, it might have been John, pointed out it might have been named after the players of the sport of curling, as there had been a curling rink round at Atholl Gardens at some time in the dim and distant past. That made sense.

John needs a rest, but not this one!

It has been claimed that T*he Curlers Rest* has been on its present site since the 18th century. If true, that would certainly put it in contention for the oldest pub title, but so far we have found nothing to back up this claim, other than the fact that the pub building is obviously much older than most of the others in the area.

The Curlers has undergone a transformation in more recent times. Where once it had been a fine old traditional pub, serving good cheer to the local community, and the odd curler. It has, in my humble and personal opinion, become an upmarket, cheerless shell of a place. Every stick of furniture, every traditional fixture and every fitting has been gutted from the place, along with any hint of character.

I really hate pubs where you feel like you should be wiping your feet before entering. With *The Curlers Rest* I wouldn't have been surprised if we had been asked to take our shoes off.

We did manage to chat to the barman for a little while, but being new to the pub and Australian he couldn't tell us much about the history of T*he Curlers*.

What he did tell us was something we didn't really want to hear. The price of the drink in this place was extortionate, so much so that for my second drink I only had a half pint. I'm fairly sure these West End prices were meant to keep the likes of me and John from lowering the tone of the place. If that is true then in this instance it worked very well. By the time we finished our drinks I couldn't have cared less about how old this pub was; I just wanted out of it.

John's comments: I imagine my comments will be similar to Craig's. This may be a fairly old pub, but not one that I would spend a lot of time in. It is for the young, upwardly mobile. I hope that makes sense as I'm not sure exactly what it means, but I'll no be back. Having said that, for young people it is a lovely pub, so don't be put off by the ramblings of two old boozers.

John's 2nd Pub; *The Laurieston*; Now we're talking about a pub, a real pub, with real ale! Now I'm sure I've criticized pubs that sell real ale, but in this pub it is just a side issue for the odd tourist or the students and other youngsters who visit on their way round on the sub-crawl. For anyone who does not know what the sub-crawl is, you go round on the Glasgow Underground, or Subway to the locals, getting off at each station, and having a drink at the nearest pub. That's 15 pints, and when you think how narrow some of the platforms on the underground are, it's amazing more kids don't fall off them and get run over.

The reason I picked *The Laurieston* as one of my oldest pubs is that I have visited it before. A couple of years ago, Kate's cousin Carine and her husband Ady were up in Scotland for a holiday. They live in Scarborough, but they love Scotland and come up as often as they can. Carine is Scottish, but has lived south of the border for many years.

Anyway, Ady loves Scottish pubs and real ale, so one day when we all met in Glasgow for the women to spent a few hours shopping, Ady told me about this pub that he had visited in the past that did real ale. I wasn't that impressed, and when he told me which pub it was, I thought he was joking-he wasn't. So it was to *The Laurieston* we went for a few drinks while the wives shopped.

I remember thinking at the time that this is a real old pub which looked really great inside, but we spent so much time talking that I did not notice too much about it, other than it looked a brilliant pub and sort of old looking.

The fabulous Laurieston, on the inside at least

Now, as you all know, there can only be one, or maybe two pubs in any place that can claim, with any honesty, to be the oldest, and I'm sure Craig's first pub *Sloans* has a strong claim in that department. But I like writing about other facts about a pub's history, and if the facts I hear from the barman or locals are true, so much the better.

It's an easy run on the Number 6 bus from just outside Craig's house. We got off just opposite the Citizen's Theatre and wandered along Bridge Street and in we went.

It had been pouring when we walked from the Citizens Theatre to the pub and we were soaked when we went in. Right away the barman came over with paper napkins to help us dry out. We knew right away this was a good bar. But did it have any claim to be the oldest in any of my categories, which, to be fair, are many and varied.

The barman, John Clancy, owns the bar along with his brother James. John's son Joseph was behind the bar with John. James had a day off today.

Once we had taken in the surrounds of the bar, which are fantastic, John came over to serve us. When we told him the reason for the visit, John spent most of the time we were in telling us stories about the history of the place. And it was a lot, as we must have had about half a dozen rounds.

One of the first things I mentioned to John was that I had heard from a local in a previous bar we had visited that *The Laurieston* has a nationally important historic interior. 'What the hell are you talking about? I hear you say. Well, this guy said that the pub has the oldest 'Island Style' bar in Glasgow, if not the whole of Scotland!! If that doesn't make it a shoo-in for this book, I don't know what does, so back to today's visit. John was honest enough to tell me that the bar had been altered slightly and was not a complete Island Bar.

This just means that *The Laurieston* is the oldest pub in Glasgow with an Island Bar which is not a complete island. That works for me. John's stories about the history of this bar, and about half a dozen other bars his family have owned were endless, and all true.

Craig finds his true spiritual home

Since this book is supposed to be about oldest boozers facts, some of the ones I collected from John and Joseph about *The Laurieston,* ones that I saw with my own eyes included: the oldest toilets with a fabulous Ceramic Tiled floor: the oldest genuine Formica topped bar, the oldest hand crafted tables and chairs fitted into bar corners, again with Formica tops. I could go on for hours about this pub and its fixtures and fittings, almost all of them carried out by John, but space is limited. You must visit and see for yourselves.

The unique decor of The Laurieston plus one old wino

The reason John can do all this craftsmanship is that as a boy he trained as a Shop-fitter, and, when he was young, one of the pubs his father owned, *The Happy Haven,* I think it was called (there was so many) needed to be expanded, so his dad bought the we flat next door and got John to re-build it into a Lounge Bar. Talk about slave labour. Anyway, the old man had not thought about planning permission and the police put a stop to it all. Most of the fixtures in *The Laurieston* come from previous pubs the family owned.

John's fame for not leaving anything of worth behind in a bar he was selling was highlighted by one of the locals beside us. He was telling the story of a guy who shouted at John as he was locking up a bar he was leaving for the last time that he had forgotten the wallpaper. I think he was kidding.

The pub is also a bit of an institution with famous sportsmen and actors. Amongst the mug shots that adorned the walls was none other than Ewan McGregor. So if you visit, you never know who you'll bump into, probably Craig and me as we liked it so much.

It was time to go as we were getting to the stage that if we didn't go right away, we would have been there all night. Hope you all agree that *The Laurieston* is in the book by right.

Craig's comments: *I don't know how he did it but I feel that John has conned me. It's all very well looking for the oldest pub in whichever town we happen to be in but is also good to find the really good ones which don't quite have the history to be eligible for that title.* The Laurieston *is one such pub. He claims to have come up with this pub simply by accident. In fact he almost apologised for picking it, saying he needed it to make up the numbers. Aye, that'll be right!*

Because John chose The Laurieston, *knowing full well that it was nowhere near being the oldest pub in Glasgow, he thought I would be obliged to pick holes in his choice, slag off the facilities and generally mock him for being daft enough to choose it in the first place. Well I refuse! I don't care that it was probably built less than a hundred years ago or that it is not mentioned in any history books. I liked it, and he knew I would.*

From outside I would have to say that the pub is less than impressive. It doesn't help that the main West Coast Railway line passes by only a few yards from the front door or that all the traffic coming up into the city from Ayrshire and beyond comes to a screeching halt at the traffic lights right outside the building. The overall effect of that is a bit depressing and, if you add to that the fact that on the day we visited the place the rain was absolutely stoating down, you can imagine that my initial impression was less than enthusiastic.

97

As soon as we set foot inside the pub I forgot about all of that nonsense. The Laurieston has to be one of the best pubs I've ever been in.

The pub has changed little in the last 50 years. It was like stepping back in time. The bar is covered in Formica and the flooring is bare wood. In fact everything about the place could have been part of a period film set.

The gaffer, John Cavell, told us that the pub had indeed been used by film studios, the most notable recent production being 'Young Adam', starring Ewan MacGregor.

The credit for keeping The Lauriston firmly rooted in this period must go to John who has a very much hands-on approach to decor and maintenance.

Scottish pub cuisine in one picture

Almost everything in the pub, nailed down or otherwise, has been either created or adapted by John. I suggested to him that maybe he should be getting a council rebate for all the recycling he has done over the years or maybe a wee backhander from

98

Historic Scotland for taking such good care of a unique example of a traditional Scottish beer shop.

In keeping with the 50s theme the only food on offer is the great Scottish pie, plain or, for the more adventurous, onion. All served from an original 1950s, glass panelled pie heating machine.

We had intended checking out one more pub on our day out, but I'm afraid that, because of a combination of good beer great company and easy access to the pie machine, we decided just to stay where we were for the rest of the day.

In short, although nowhere near being the oldest boozer in toon, I would admit that The Laurieston *could well be in contention for the title of best in toon.*

John: Our final pub of the day, *The Laurieston,* was just a short walk across to the Citizens Theatre, then we got the 18 bus back to EK. We felt no pain as it was a brilliant day.

Find oor Auld Boozers

by Bus . . . .

If you don't know how to get to Glasgow, we're no telling you.

. . . . then by Boot

Sloan's
On Argyle Street just inside the Argyle Arcade on the left.

The Three Judges
On Dumbarton Road at the bottom of Byres Road. This is well worth a visit, especially if you are a boxing fan, or even a Thistle fan.

The Curlers
On Byres Road, just up past the Underground Station on the same side of the Road.

The Laurieston
On the corner of Bridge Street and Nelson Street, just over the King George IV Bridge. Many people (fearties) and some tourists, may be put off by where the pub is to be found. Although it's only about a 10 minute walk from the Centre of Glasgow, just go over the KG5 bridge and it's a couple of hundred yards on your right, it's not the most salubrious area in our garden city, but it's worth the effort.

Kirkcaldy

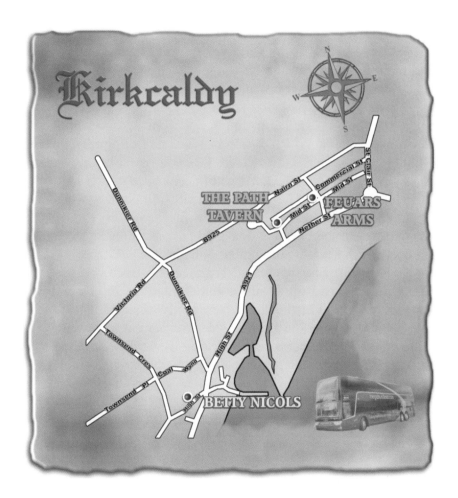

John: Kirkcaldy, we call it the back-to-front town. In most coastal towns, the seafront is the nicest part of the town and the back of the town is usually hidden away, but not Kirkcaldy. It's a lovely town until you get down to the front, then jings, crivvens and help ma boab! Mind you, we only visit the town centre bit of the front. It might improve further out? It couldn't get any worse.

Many years ago, Kirkcaldy was known as 'The Lang Toun' after the mile-long main street. Thought you would all like to know that little bit of history.

Today's trip was an epic to arrange. Waterstone's in Perth wanted some books, as did Kirkcaldy, so the idea was to deliver to Perth and Kirkcaldy in the one day, as well as trying to find the oldest pub in Kirkcaldy. It was Craig who came up with the idea of me leaving EK early in the morning, getting a bus to Perth, delivering the books, then getting a bus from Perth which would take me to a 'Park and Ride' stop just outside Dunfermline, where I would get on the direct bus from Glasgow to Kirkcaldy, which, hopefully, he would be on, after getting a long lie!

This sounded like a nightmare; God knows where we would end up. But this is part of the fun and helps to keep me young. So with the planning done and the pieces made, I ventured out on a dreich Friday morning full of hope.

The 'keeping me young' bit doesn't seem to be working. Today, in my rush to get on the bus, I gave the lady bus driver what I thought was my bus pass. It was only when she asked me to enter my pin number did I realize I'd given her the wrong card.

As I'm getting older, I'm getting worse. I remember in my working days travelling all over Europe and America without too much difficulty. Nowadays, it's a challenge even to get on the No. 18 bus without screwing up.

Luckily, after that wee problem, the remainder of the journey passed without a hitch. I delivered the books to the Perth branch of Waterstone's and my next bus met up with Craig's X26 at Halbeath Park and Ride just outside Dunfermline. By the way, the Fife Council must have been a bit flush when they built the Park and Ride. There must be enough stops for about eight buses at a time. Maybe they think there is going to be a big expansion in bus travel in the future. Who knows!

After delivering our books to the Kirkcaldy store, we headed to the first of three pubs Craig had researched on the web. But as always, I would follow the advice of the locals in the first pub we visited before deciding on my pub. So we ventured into his first choice.

Craig's 1st pub: *Betty Nicol's.* We had been to this pub before and I wasn't too sure that we should be going back there. I thought that we knew as much as we were ever going to about the place. As it turned out it was well worth our while making a return journey.

Betty's is only a few hundred yards along the road from Waterstone's bookshop, so it was an ideal starting point for us.

We had just dropped off another consignment of our latest highly successful book and we thought that we deserved a bit of a refreshment.

According to my sources, i.e. the internet, Betty Nicol's had a good claim to being the oldest pub in Kirkcaldy. When we started out researching material for this book I had a lot of faith in the results obtained from the net. It hasn't taken very long for that faith to be dented somewhat.

It would appear that the internet is inhabited by various groups of nutters, morons and the deluded. Take my advice, if you ever need to use the internet, only believe about 10 per cent of information which spews out of it.

As my first choice pub in Kirkcaldy *Betty Nicol's* certainly looks the part. From the outside the pub looks to be a classic example of an early Scottish drinking establishment. Inside it is every bit as traditional, with bare floorboards and stained-glass windows. There are also tiled areas at the entrances and around the bar.

Although the seating areas have obviously been updated over the years, the overall effect gives the impression of an old but perfectly preserved ale house.

It's just a pity that it's all a fake. It seems that the present day pub is an exact replica of the original pub which was built on that site in 1741. That pub was called *The Victoria Bar* and over the years it changed hands several times. For reasons which were never explained the present day pub was built in 1902

Betty's has known a number of names in its time, including *The Victoria Bar*, *The Victoria* and, for some bizarre reason *The Fun Pub*.

This latter incarnation came about sometime in the 1980s, a time often referred to as the decade fashion forgot. Apparently all of the tiled surfaces and wall panels were boarded over and garishly painted. Fortunately, sense prevailed and the pub was returned to its former glory within a short time.

Betty Nicols, Kirkcaldy

Our barmaid, Joyce Mackie, told us, after a little encouragement, about some ghostly goings on in the pub. One morning not so long ago the pub cleaner turned up to do her shift. As usual, she let herself in and started doing whatever it is that cleaners do. When she entered the back area of the pub she was shocked to find a tea light candle still burning on one of the tables.

I think Joyce must have seen the look on my face, the look that said, 'So what?' She quietly explained that because they are so small tea lights cannot last more than a couple of hours at most. Therefore it shouldn't or couldn't still be alight eight hours after the pub closed. It could only be the work of a restless spirit.

104

John was very impressed by this but I thought it was a bit less than scary. Just how menacing can an evil presence be if it is afraid of the dark?

There are however other reports of ghosts wandering around the bar. Joyce herself has felt their presence. She told us that there have been sightings down in the pub cellar. Apparently most of the barmaids are none too keen to go down there to get extra stock for the bar.

Things got to such a state that the owners brought in a psychic investigator to check the pub out for malevolent spirits. After an extensive search the investigator concluded that there were indeed signs of ghosts in all areas of the pub.

Joyce shared some ghostly stories

One of the customers told me that the bloke spent as much time trying to flog his book to them as he did investigating. I said that this was disgusting abuse of his position and I would definitely be saying something about it in our forthcoming book, *The Auldest Boozers in Toon*, competitively priced at £8.99 and available from all Waterstone's book stores.

I do know that John was definitely having a bit of a problem with spirits. Today was one of his vodka and soda days and his problem was that the optic measure in Betty's was only 25ml. He really hates that. His solution to the problem of what he refers to as 'short measures' was to sneak in a fly one whenever he thought I wasn't looking. Of course as the day went on he got less and less fly.

It was time to move on to our next pub. Hopefully it would be of historical interest and for the sake of our limited resources I really hoped it would have 35ml spirit measures.

Joyce told us that there were two other pubs quite close by which were of a good age. She even gave us detailed directions to them. But I could tell that she was less than convinced that we would ever see them. As it turned out, it would have served my purposes better if we hadn't found the first of them.

John's comments: I'm not sure if the original date of 1741 can be taken too seriously. The pub has changed names and owners more often than I've had hot dinners. It is a very nice pub though and the staff and regulars were good company.

An old guy sitting on his own in the corner of the bar shouted me over when he heard what we were doing. There was nothing up with his hearing, though I never said that to him. He was a great old guy, and when I asked him if he knew of any pubs older than Bettys, *he told me that there was a wee pub just a short walk along the road and up a wee hill, called* 'Path Tavern', *which he reckoned was the oldest in the town. That was good enough for me. I told Craig just as we were about to leave that I had chosen my pub.*

Craig was knackered by the time we had done the 'wee' walk. I didn't care, as the pub looked interesting from the outside, so after waiting about 20 minutes for Craig to take his customary photo of the pub, in we went.

John's 1st pub: *The Path Tavern;* The sign on the outside of the building said it was built in 1730, so I knew I was on to a winner right away, in my mind anyway. Craig reminded me that was the date when the building was built, not when a pub was opened. He knows how to kill the moment.

106

Although my first impression when glancing through the window was of someone's living room, as soon as we entered the pub, I liked it. There was a great atmosphere in the place and the bar itself was brilliant. It was solid wood and built in the shape of a snake. Not a coiled up snake, but like the letter 'S', really unusual, and it's worth visiting the pub just to stand at the bar.

It was an all-girl lineup behind the bar and kitchen. Julie Philip and Heather Davidson were good company and told us as much as they knew about the history of the pub. It was a pity the owner, George Mackay, was not in or we would have found out more, but we did find out from the two girls and the 'Kitchen Scrubber', Julie Murray, that the pub had been in existence since 1730, as stated on the building.

We were on the right path heading for this pub

One of the locals I was talking to showed me a poster on the wall which told the story of a local baker called Andrew Wilson. Now Andrew did a bit of smuggling and was fed up with the Revenue men taking too much tax, which he reckoned all went south to the English. To cut a long story short, Andrew and his pals robbed the Revenue Men, were caught, escaped and were eventually killed and buried behind the pub. I think, like most of my stories, they are told to me after a few pints, but stories like that are part of the history of the town.

Funnily enough, in our previous pub, I heard Craig talking to some local about smugglers. The locals must have had a flair for smuggling. Maybe they used that flair for laying the Linoleum for which the town became famous.

As we said our goodbyes and were leaving, I noticed a great sign on the door which said, '*mind, you're working tomorrow*'. I liked that.

Julie and Heather explain the big words to John

'*The Path*' is a great wee pub, which qualifies for its position in this book because even if, it was not the oldest pub in the town, it has the oldest 'snake bar' in town, and well worth the walk to get there. I'm sure there is a bus you could get during the day. They were all off by the time we left our next pub, Craig's second, which was just round the corner.

Craig's comments: *The one thing Joyce didn't tell us was that for us to get to* The Path Tavern *we would have to scale a miniature mountain. Well it felt like a bit of a climb to me. But it was well worth the effort to reach such a fine pub.*

As far as it being the oldest pub in Kirkcaldy is concerned the only evidence we could find was the inscription above the front door. If it really was opened in 1730, then I would have to concede that John, by complete chance, had found the town's oldest boozer,

108

and therefore I had yet again backed a loser in the historical pub stakes.

Craig's 2nd pub: *Feuars:* My second pub of the day was *The Feuars Arms*. Fortunately it was only a short walk from The Path. Once again we had found a striking looking public house.

The Feuars is an A listed building, meaning that no structural changes are allowed. To be honest it is hard to imagine how anyone could change a building like this one. It is so substantial that it would probably take explosives to even put a dent in it. It is truly unique.

Out on the tiles in the Feuars Arms

However, being unique doesn't necessarily mean pretty. I didn't really like the look of the place as we approached it. You don't often see a turreted pub in Scotland, certainly not in a housing scheme in the middle of Kirkcaldy. To me it seemed a bit out of place,

The pub's address is a bit on the unique side as well. Bogies Wynd. Maybe 'bogies' has a different meaning on the East coast.

If we thought the outside was a bit unusual we were shocked at what we found inside. The entire floor was covered in high quality ceramic tiles. In fact almost every surface in the place seemed to be tiled, including the bar.

I think I said something to the effect that I felt as if we were standing in the middle of the world's biggest and fanciest toilet. The barman misheard me and gave us directions to the Gents. John didn't want the direction to go to waste and scurried off to find them. He does have a bit of a bladder problem after all. I suppose you could call it a wee problem.

When he came back he raved about the décor in the toilet. Apparently the mosaic tiled theme continued on the floor in there. The urinals are framed in white marble and the cisterns are glass-fronted. They must be very special indeed as he said they were almost as fancy as the Victorian toilets on the pier of his beloved Rothesay.

Ian and Liz try hard to ignore John

Back in the bar we chatted to Ian and Liz Smith, who are big fans of The Feuar, its décor and its history.

The pub was originally a flour mill before being converted into a pub in 1859. Thirty years later it was completely rebuilt and has remained pretty much untouched since its last remodelling in 1902.

There are three large stained-glass windows around the pub depicting the coats of arms of Scotland, England and Ireland. Apparently no one knows why Wales was omitted from this lineup but it would seem reasonable to assume that it might have had something to do with the nationality of the original owners.

On the tiled wall of the pub two tiled paintings can be seen. They are by Doulton's of Lambeth and the only similar ones can be found in the St James Tavern, London

The rather odd shaped bar is 59 feet in length and has a massive mahogany gantry in the middle.

Although I appreciated all of the history on display in the bar, to be honest it was all a bit too much for me and what John would call my simple tastes. It didn't feel like a real pub to me. I half expected to see tour guides leading tourists around the place.

I did enjoy the beer and the company, even John's, but I just thought there was a lack of atmosphere in the place. Too much museum, not enough pub.

Added to that was the fact that John's choice of pub was almost certainly older than mine.

John's comments: This is a really unusual looking pub, both from the outside and inside. The place is a cross between a Victorian toilet and the Vatican. You probably have no idea what I'm talking about. You will just have to go and see for yourself. It is worth a visit, but I don't think it's as old as 'The Path'.

John: Homeward bound; three old pubs were visited today, and I think *The Path* qualifies as the oldest, but I might be wrong. Does it really matter?

The journey home was not without incident. By the time we left Kirkcaldy, there were no direct buses to Glasgow, so after a bit of a panic, we found out that we could get a bus to Dunfermline and change there. In Dunfermline we had about an hour to kill, so they were killed in a local pub, which to Craig's horror, turned out to be a Wetherspoon's. But the drink is cheap and we had no time to find anywhere else.

When we left the pub, I had no idea of the way back to the Bus Station and took a right when it should have been left.

Eventually, about a minute before the last bus to Glasgow was due to leave, I asked a few youngsters how to get to the station. They were fantastic, and took us physically by the arms and we all ran to the station. The girl that helped me talked the driver into waiting a few minutes so Craig would not miss the bus. Craig does not do running; even walking is a challenge. About 20 minutes later when he got his breath back, he gave me dog's abuse for getting lost. Thank God he fell asleep. We both did and only wakened when the bus turned into Buchanan Street Bus Station.

Find oor Auld Boozers

by Bus . . . .

The X26 Glasgow to Leven from Buchanan Street Bus Station takes you all the way to Kirkcaldy Bus Station..

. . . . then by Boot

Betty Nicols
You come out of the bus station and walk down towards the sea. When you get to High Street, which is only about a hundred yards or so from the bus station, take a left and the pub is about a five minute walk, it's on the left side of the street.

The Path Tavern
Turn left when you leave *Betty Nicol's.* You continue along the road and up the hill. At the top take a left and you'll see the pub in front of you. It's about a 10 minute walk (20 if you're with Craig).

Feuars Pub
Turn left when you leave 'The Path Tavern' and it's the first street on the left. You will see it from the corner.

Roamin Roon Loch Lomond

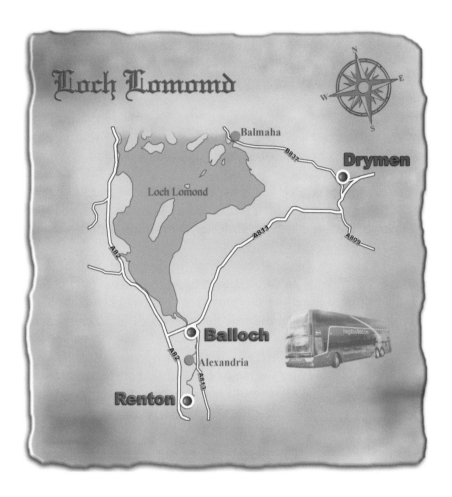

John: The Loch Lomond area is one of the nicest and most famous in Scotland, and Craig in particular thought it was important we visited it. I thought he must have an ulterior motive for this interest; I had my suspicions.

It's a big area to cover, so we would have to do it in more than one visit, but this is ok as we have plenty of time, and the buses are free.

Shortly before the first of our visits to the area, Craig said we should visit Drymen as he thought there may be a really old pub there.

Drymen is not a big city, or even a big town, or even a big village, but seemingly it has a big claim to have the oldest pub in Scotland, and Craig wanted to have it as his first pub in the Loch Lomond area. I went along with this as I don't really care where we go as long as I can have a good day out and a wee refreshment when we get there, wherever it is.

The pub in Drymen with the 'oldest' claim is called *The Clachan Inn* and it has been registered as licensed premises since 1734. So a visit was needed to try and find out if their claim is justified.

Drymen is only a few miles from the shores of Loch Lomond at Balmaha, and a nicer part of the country would be hard to find. I think it is on the route of 'The West Highland Way', so the only downside is that the place might be full of hikers with the big boots and backpacks filling the place. Only time would tell.

As usual, I had the task of organizing the buses, so, after checking the 'Traveline' website, I found that there were only a couple of buses a day that would get you there or back in a waney (no changes needed). The one to Drymen was too early in the morning even for Craig and me to have a bevy, but there was a direct one back at about half five in the evening, so I planned the journey in reverse.

To get the five thirty bus back, we would want to get there in time for at least three hours to check the place out, have a wee bevy and see if there were other wee boozers in the village. So I planned for a bus leaving Glasgow about 12 o'clock. This would go via Balloch where we would change buses twice and end up in Drymen about one thirty. I know you can work out that this would be four hours in Drymen, but an extra hour in a wee old bar is neither here nor there, and as it turned out, we needed the extra time.

It would also let us check out the pubs in Balloch, as it is on the loch and probably the biggest town on it.

We left EK in time to arrive in Buchanan Street Bus Station by 11.40am to get the 11.55am number 926 City Link bus to just outside Balloch, where Loch Lomond starts. Where all going to plan, we would cross the road, the A82, and catch McGills No. 305 which goes from Luss into Balloch. It says it's only three minutes, but it looks like a big walk into the Bus Terminus in Balloch. From there we would get the McGills No. 309 to Drymen. It's a complex plan and one I was proud of, but with my track record it would go belly up at some point, but that's part of the fun, that, and watching Craig's reaction to another foul up.

Having said all that, I had a minor concern about the old 926 bus route. It goes from Glasgow all the way to Campbeltown, which, as many of you will know, is a downer for Craig. The number of times he has been thwarted from reaching Campbeltown because of bus delays caused by landslides on the 'Rest and be Thankful', or cowardice on the part of the captain of the 'Waverley' are legendary, well in Craig's mind anyway. Even the day we did reach Campbeltown by bus, it took over six hours and we only had a couple of hours to sample the local pubs. It took Craig weeks to recover.

I decided to play it safe and book us seats on the bus. I also decided not to tell Craig what route we were on till we were at the bus station. Anything for a quiet life!

We arrived at the bus station in plenty of time to catch the infamous Campbeltown service. Craig was not to be fooled; he clocked right away what service we were getting. The big sign saying Campbeltown on the front of the bus was a giveaway. To be fair, it was a glorious day and even Craig was mellow in his remarks about my choice of route. He had noticed however, that we had only about six minutes between getting of this bus and catching our next one for the short three minute run into Balloch.

The CCC (Craig's Campbeltown Curse) struck immediately. The bus was 10 minutes late leaving Glasgow and never made up the time. My saying that the next bus might be late didn't help. We got off our bus just after the big roundabout at the bottom of Loch Lomond and spent about 20 minutes trying to cross the road, it was a nightmare. Eventually we made it. There was no sign of the next bus, and checking the timetable at the stop, the next bus was tomorrow. Craig's criticism was muted because a bloke had got off the bus with us and was following us. He had been sitting in front of us and it was obvious he had no idea where he was. We thought he was foreign. It turned out he was. We asked him at the bus stop if we could help him. We could. He was over from Northern Ireland on a short trip on his own to get out of the place. We were almost at the 12th of July and he said home could be a wee bit lively at this time of year.

When we asked him where he was going he said Drymen! What are the chances of that! We thought he had heard us talking on the bus and was taking the piss, but it turned out when we told him that's where we were going he thought we were doing the same to him. We showed him our paperwork for the journey and I think he was a bit relieved. What did he think two pensioners were going to do-kidnap him!

His name was Nigel McLuchie, a real nice bloke. He told us he wanted a bit of a quiet time for a few days to have a wee think about his future. He was between jobs. He was thinking of going to China to teach English as he had done a bit of teaching in the past. I told him he was brave to go all that way on his own. What I actually said was 'Gaun yourself China', but nobody laughed. He was actually heading for Rowardennan and had booked accommodation in the hostel there. We sorted him out on how to get there.

By the time we had done all that meeting and organizing we had walked almost all the way to the bus terminus in Balloch and Craig had forgotten he was in a bad mood. We checked up on the bus times and realized we had an hour and a half to wait for the next No. 309 to Drymen.

Our experience in situations like this (screw-ups) meant we knew right away what to do. The extra time would let us not only check out Balloch, but we would have the time to visit the oldest pub. As Craig had 'bagged' the pub in Drymen, I said that I would take whatever pub we picked in Balloch.

Nigel said he would love to join us, so we wandered back into town and it didn't take us long to find what looked like the oldest pub in town, *The Dog House*, so in we went.

John's Balloch Pub: *The Dog House.* It was a great wee pub and the barman Andy McGregor was a young and very helpful barman. The locals, on the other hand, were a crazy bunch, the kind of people we get on with. But first we had to confirm my thoughts that this was Balloch's oldest pub. Andy and the crazy locals all agreed it was the oldest and could date it back to 'long ago', their words. This would do for me so we settled in to get some background of this great pub.

John sniffs out Balloch's oldest pub

Craig's first impression of the pub was not as enthusiastic as mine, he even complained to the barman about a carpeted area near the door. Carpets are on Craig's list of things he hates in pubs.

117

His opinion soon changed when Andy told him that he discouraged children and that very few women ever came in. Craig's change of heart was complete when he discovered that a pint was only £2.80. He even suggested that I should carry on to Drymen and he would settle in *The Dog* and have a quiet afternoon. I reminded him that he was not here to enjoy himself. We were supposed to be working.

I was still sober, so I thought I would try a bit harder to find out an exact date when the pub opened. Now Craig and I differ on what Andy might have said. I'm sure he said it opened in the 1870s, but Craig says that what he said was that it opened in the 70s. Craig's insistence on historical accuracy can be a bit tedious.

Barman Andy keeps the booze hounds well supplied

Another historically important fact about *The Dog* is that it has raised thousands of pounds over the years for charity, for a longer time than any other pub in Balloch. Now that's something to be proud of, and another reason it should feature in this book.

The locals we met, Davie (Ding Dong) Bell, who is the pub's bowls champion, Alex Davidson and some other crazies kept us going with their facts and stories about the pub and its regulars.

While we were chatting to the locals about their charity work, I noticed a great big Labrador lying under the table enjoying a bowl of lager (it was a very hot day). The guys told me the dog played a big role in their charity work. I was intrigued and asked what it did. According to one of them, the Lab was a retired guide dog who did a bit of part-time work guiding his new owner from one hole to the other on the golf course. When I enquired if the gentleman was blind, the answer I got was 'yes, blind drunk most of the time'. Even the dog seemed to be laughing at me. Sometimes I can be a bit gullible.

I don't know what Nigel was thinking about all this, but he said he was having a great time and it reminded him of home. God knows what home must be like, although, come to think on it, Northern Ireland is full of crazies. Must arrange a visit soon.

Time for our next bus was approaching so we said goodbye to the locals and the oldest pub in Balloch, or is it?

Craig's comments: The Dog House *looked like the ideal pub for us, it was near the bus station and it was open. The bar is fairly traditional although there is a carpeted area near the door. Obviously I complained about this to the barman and he apologised immediately. In his defence he did point out that children were discouraged from entering the bar and very few women ever came in.*

When I found out that my pint of lager only cost £2.80 I suggested to John that he should continue on to Drymen and I would keep a space at the bar for him until he got back. He thought I was kidding and I was forced to humour him.

John interviewed our barman, asking him if the Dog was the oldest pub in Balloch. The lad looked a bit puzzled and said he thought it had been built in the 70s. Ignoring all evidence to the contrary John insisted he meant the 1870s. The barman tried to set him straight but John was having none of it. He likes a bit of history does John, even if he has to make it up himself.

I suggested to him that if he intended making the bar trade his career he may like to practise being a bit more economical with the truth. In this instance when a booze-befuddled senior-

citizen makes outrageous claims, the bar person may consider just shrugging his or her shoulders and mumbling 'could be'. That would keep everybody happy.

I have to say that once the effects of the sun and the booze wore off John admitted that The Dog House was not in any way a contender for the oldest pub. I think I helped him come to this realisation when I pointed out that he had jackets older than this pub.

Craig's 1st Drymen Pub: *The Clachan Inn*; We walked the couple of hundred yards to the bus terminal and our next bus, McGill's No. 309 arrived on time and we fairly belted up the road to Drymen.

Our Irish friend Nigel was staying on the bus to Rowardennan, so we said our goodbyes, and wished him all the best for a flute free couple of days.

The bus dropped us off 100 yards from our main pub of the day, *The Clachan Inn*. This great wee country pub sits at the far end of the Village Green in Drymen. The Clachan Inn is the oldest pub in Scotland, or so it claims, and it has been serving up ale since 1730.

The Clachan, Drymen

Actually that is where things get a bit confused. The pub bases its claim on the fact that it was the first registered pub in Scotland. Back then the government decided that all Inns and Ale Houses needed to be registered. Presumably this was another tax raising scam which probably required the licencee to part with a large bag of cash. Of course there were thousands of pubs doing a roaring trade for centuries before the government got greedy.

Interestingly, the first licencee of this pub was a woman who just happened to be the sister of legendary cattleman Rob Roy MacGregor. Unlike his sister, Rob wasn't over keen on paperwork, often misplacing the bill of sale for the herd of cattle he 'owned'. In fact no one was ever quite sure just how many cows he 'owned' at any given time.

The village of Drymen is just three miles from Loch Lomond and centuries ago it was the mustering point and market place for cattle brought down from the Highlands. From there the herds journeyed on down to the big meat market at Smithfield, London.

Drymen was the natural gathering point for most of the small cattle herds as The Endrick River, which flows into Loch Lomond, has its lowest crossing point, just outside the village. This meant that the cows could easily and safely be driven across the ford. The onward journey down to London could take up to eight weeks.

This made Drymen a popular place for drovers to stop for provisions and of course the odd refreshment. I suppose it could be said that Rob Roy's sister might quickly rustle up some food for the drovers in her busy little Inn while her brother was busy out and about doing a bit of rustling of his own.

Actually it might just be that he had to put the pub in his sister's name in case the licensing authorities took a dim view of his late night cattle relocation scheme.

Amanda Goode, our barmaid, told us that *The Clachan* gets a lot of passing trade from the hardy types who trek the length of The West Highland Way. Apparently there is another, less well known, long distance walk which starts from the middle of

Drymen. The Rob Roy Way stretches from the village to Pitlochry, a total of 92 miles.

Added to that, Drymen also reaps the benefit of being in The Loch Lomond and The Trossachs National Park, with many tourists exploring the area.

There were only three other customers in the bar while we were there. But that was more than enough for John to cause a wee bit of chaos. There is an unwritten rule, one that really needs to be written down, which states that alcohol and politics don't mix.

Either John has never heard of the rule or the alcohol snuck up on him. As an avid reader of The Daily Mail, and an even more avid imbiber of strong drink, John's strange political outlook has led us into to some interesting situations in the past. Sometimes those interesting situations could be better described as scary and today was one of those times.

It all started quite innocently, with some fairly bland bar chatter. Unfortunately John was just getting into gear.

To set the scene, it was about four weeks before the Independence Referendum and John was returning to his Tory roots. An increasingly angry bloke at the bar wasn't too keen on listening to John's theory on us all being 'Better Together'.

Amanda with a couple of Clachaners

Invoking the memory of the late, and universally unlamented, Margaret Thatcher to illustrate his point didn't do much to calm this bloke down. I was torn between listening in to the conversation and checking the bar out for emergency exits.

Being a couple of sheets to the wind John had failed to notice the throbbing vein on the bloke's forehead. Things were looking bad. I was reminded of that old story about the two guys who find themselves confronted by a Grizzly Bear. One of them asks his pal, "Do you think you can outrun a bear?" His mate replies, "I don't need to run faster than the bear, I just need to run faster than you". Given I was the one with the dodgy knees I feared the worst.

Fortunately for us the bloke decided that storming out of the pub muttering what sounded like a critical appraisal of our worth as Scotsmen was the best way to make his point. It all went a bit quiet after that so we had a few more drinks to celebrate not getting our heads pummelled.

As usual we decided to make a day of it by visiting one more pub before making our way home. 'The Winnock' is only about fifty yards away from *The Clachan*, but miles away in style.

Despite the closeness of our next port of call one of the blokes we had been talking to offered his services as a guide. I think he must have been matching John drink for drink since he admitted later that this was his first visit to Drymen.

John's comments: *The Clachan may lay claim to being old, and it certainly is an old looking place, but to be honest, I liked* The Dog House *better. When I told Craig this he told me what I liked had nothing to do with the book as we were trying to trace the oldest pub. And here was me thinking he was in a good mood. Mind you, he wasn't the only one who was grumpy; one of the locals who was a fanatical 'Yes' to independence man took exception to me trying to take the piss out of him. What's life if you can't have a laugh at politics? I was glad to escape the place.*

123

Craig's 2nd Drymen Pub: *The Winnock Hotel*; Although a good age, our third pub of the day has never, to my knowledge, made any extravagant claims to be a front runner in the oldest pub stakes.

The Winnock Hotel has developed to its present size over many years. Originally it was made up of a row of cottages and has gradually been added to. The first part of the building has been dated to sometime in the late 1700s. Nowadays it is a busy hotel catering for the increasing tourist trade which has been generated by the opening of the long distance walks through the area. Added to that, *The Winnock* is ideally placed to take advantage of the increasing numbers of visitors to The National Park.

The Drymen Ceilidh Centre

Apparently regular Ceilidhs and Scottish Nights are held in *The Winnock*. Despite this I still quite liked the place. I can just about understand the draw of a Ceilidh, lots of drinking and spinning around to music, but the concept of a Scottish Night escapes me.

To be a truly Scottish night do they expect their customers to drink between eight and ten pints of lager, pick a fight with a total stranger, and leave half a kebab in their jacket pocket overnight. I really can't see that catching on with foreign tourists.

The décor of the place, as you would expect, suggests its Scottish heritage, but in a very modern way. Perhaps I just don't move in the right circles, but it all looked a bit false and too upmarket for my liking. That being said it is very well finished and is a comfortable place to visit.

And we had timed our visit to perfection. Three o'clock on a Wednesday afternoon in July is the perfect time to enjoy a quiet pint in *The Winnock*. The place was entirely tourist free.

I assumed that the hotel guests must have all been out enjoying their Scottish experience. Things like shooting defenceless animals, catching fish they were never going to eat and ruining pleasant forest trails with their £1,000 mountain bikes.

Gordon bends yet another font

Anyway, whatever they were doing, the point was, they weren't doing it in the bar of the hotel and that suited us just fine.

Without so much as an accordion sound track playing in the background we chatted to our barman, a huge guy called Gordon Stewart, and enjoyed a couple of ice cold beers. It was a pleasant way to end our day out in the Loch Lomond area.

John's comments: Although not claiming to be any great age, I liked the pub and the barman was a nice big bloke. If you're in the area and voted 'No', you won't get the same abuse as you'll get in The Clachan.

John: Our bus home, the C8, took us straight back to Glasgow. That is, straight back after visiting every nook and cranny between Drymen and the city. We slept most of the way.

Craig and I had a meeting the next day in our local. We both agreed that we should do more in the Loch Lomond area, and not just the touristy bits like Drymen and Balloch.

We decided to go from the sublime to the ridiculous. 'Why don't we try a pub in Renton', I said. I had been there once before and knew it was where the real people live. I told Craig he would love it. It's a cross between Govan and Auchinleck. But the locals are more like 'Auchinleckians', 'That bad eh', was his reply. It was also in the area where our editor Ian lives, so we asked him to join us. Ian said he had been in the pub once and it was a real old man's pub, and one of the oldest pubs in the Loch Lomond area. He tried to warn us off, but we would have none of it. So the visit was on.

It was a Saturday in June. We got the No. 18 into Glasgow and caught the First Bus No. 1 on Argyle Street, which dropped us off on the Main Street in Renton after about an hour and a quarter, which felt like about four hours.

When we got off the bus, Ian, and an old (younger than me) local called Fergus McLellan were waiting to meet us and convince us that the inside of the pub was better than the outside.

Craig said that as this was a pub where the people were akin to him (crazy), he said he wanted to cover it (write about it).

Craig's Renton Pub; I don't actually know who came up with the idea of visiting *The Central Bar* in Renton. But I do know that it wasn't me. I only have two suspects: John and our editor Ian.

Obviously one of them, or possibly both of them, came up with the idea just to test my nerves. Up until quite recently I had been blissfully unaware of the existence of Renton. And I would have been happy enough if things had remained that way.

When the suggestion to visit the place was put to me I had no idea where it was, or what kind of reputation it had, so I naively

126

assumed that it was yet another quaint old Scottish town. Only after I agreed to include it in our tour did either of my tormentors let slip that it might be a bit dodgy.

By the time we were on our way to Renton I was convinced that we were heading towards an urban wasteland. So it was a bit of a shock to find that it was a fairly pleasant little town.

Abandon hope all who enter here

We met up with Ian and his pal Fergus on the corner of Station Street and Main Street and wandered the few yards to the pub. That's when my notion of a cosy country inn went out of the window completely.

I was convinced that I had been conned once again. The building in front of us was obviously derelict. We just stood there looking at each other waiting for someone to make a suggestion as to where we might find another pub, preferably one which hadn't shut down back in the 1970s.

John, who has a knack of finding his way into pubs, noticed that the door of *The Central* was slightly ajar. Given the state of the place I suggested that the door hinges had just rusted away. But he insisted on going in to investigate. He can get very brave when he has a bit of a drouth on. A few seconds later he shouted out to us that there were people in the bar and that we should come in. It crossed my mind that the folk inside were probably squatters or vandals returning to finish off their earlier handy work.

But once inside I had to admit that the pub was indeed still in business. Not a lot of business it has to be said, but enough for our purposes.

The décor was a bit of a shock, late 19th century if I had to guess. All the proprietors since then must have been pleased with the look of the place as it doesn't seem to have been threatened by so much as a paint brush since its door first opened.

A Rosie among thorns

John, unbelievably, had done some research on *The Central Bar* before our visit and had found out that it was a listed building. Standing in the bar I couldn't help but wonder what it is listed as.

The high ceiling is decorated with some intricate plasterwork and is a deep orange colour. On closer inspection I am convinced that the ceiling would turn out to be coated in tar from many decades worth of Capstan full strength.

The bar furniture is what might be described as eclectic; it could also be called a pile of firewood which has been loosely shaped into tables and chairs.

We have visited many pubs over the years and have especially enjoyed the ones with lots of character. There may be many things wrong with *The Central Bar* but you would have to admit that it has bags of character.

Unfortunately what it didn't have bags of was beer. Fergus asked for a pint of Guinness while Ian opted for a pint of Pale Ale as his tipple of choice. The poor barmaid had to them that the only draught beer to be had in the pub was Tennent's Lager.

Not to be put off Ian asked for a wee malt whisky, only to be told that there was no such spirit in the bar. So it was Tennent's all round. At least one of us was perfectly happy.

Ian and Fregus pretend to enjoy their pints

After a couple of really good pints of lager we decided to have a word with some of the locals. I had a chat with Donald MaCeachern. To be honest, given all I had been told about the area, I thought the best I could expect would be a discussion about the shortcomings of Scottish football. Instead Donald told me all about two of Renton's most famous sons: Tobias Smollett and James Wright.

Smollett was an author and poet in the 18th century. He was a contemporary of Samuel Johnson and influenced the work of later authors such as Charles Dickens. I was very impressed.

As a student James Wright frequented The Central Bar in the late 1930s. Wright might not be immediately recognisable as a famous figure but, later in life under his pen name, James Heriot he became a household name in Britain.

I mentioned to Donald that the pub looked like nothing much had changed for a very long time. But he told me that he had a rather painful memory of one change that had taken place in the pub. Apparently he had been standing in the bar one night, talking to a friend. As they chatted he leant back against the wall without realising that a door had been put into it. Unfortunately the door had been left open. He described it as a Del Boy moment!

It was hard not to talk about the state of the pub but another of the customers suggested a possible reason for the lack of modernisation. *The Central* has been used in numerous films and television programmes in the past and is due to appear in the remake of Whisky Galore. It seems that there is money to be made from doing nothing.

Neil, Jonny and Donald

John managed a wee chat to our barmaid Rosie McCall, and she told him that she had been serving behind the bar in *The Central* for 15 years. I was tempted to say that only having the one beer and no choice of vodka must make serving pretty easy. But I didn't.

Asked if she had ever witnessed anything unusual in the bar she said that in her time behind the bar she had seen a few unbelievable sights. But like a true professional she refused to dish the dirt. Maybe we shouldn't have used the word witnessed. Renton strikes me as the kind of place where being a witness might not be the healthy option.

The one question we really needed an answer to was how old was the pub? Unfortunately that question was to go unanswered, nobody seemed to know.

However, as Fergus pointed out of all the boozers which had once graced the fair town of Renton *The Central Ba*r is the last one standing. Therefore it had to be the oldest boozer in town.

That was good enough for me, and John seemed quite satisfied as well. Of course he had been knocking back vodka all day so it was hard to tell what he was thinking.

It crossed my mind to point out that if the bar was the only one in Renton then it was both the oldest and newest boozer in town. But John looked confused enough so I kept my thoughts to myself.

__John's comments__; It's a hell of a looking pub from the outside. To get in you had to open a big heavy steel door which took all my strength. I was keeching myself. Why I was worried I have no idea, these pubs are always the best inside, and this was no exception.

Minor details, like the fact that all they had to drink was lager, whisky and vodka were not important in such a boozer. After all, if these three drinks are not enough, there's something up with you.

When I got over the shock of the inside of the place, which was hard to describe, we wandered over to the bar and were warmly welcomed by the three locals who were holding it up.

I'm sure Craig has filled you in with all the stories and traditions of the pub, but from a personal point of view, I had a great time with Fergus: A great football man and Life Member and President of the Vale of Leven Juniours. What he didn't know about Scottish Football is not worth knowing. He even knew some of the players I played alongside with the great Govan High FP's.

Although it's nothing to look at outside or in, it's a great pub and if you are ever in Renton, you're probable lost. No seriously, it's a brilliant wee pub for the more mature man, meaning old timers like Craig and I.

I tried to find out how old the pub was, hundreds of years old was the reply from all the locals. How old it really is I have no idea. But it is the oldest in Renton. Once you see it you will agree.

Find oor Auld Boozers
by Bus ....

Balloch; If, unlike us, you organise a day trip to Balloch, the No. 1 will take you from Buchanan Street Bus Station straight to Balloch.

Drymen; The No. C8 will take you from Buchanan Street Bus Station to the wee square in Drymen.

Renton; First Bus No. 1 all the way from Glasgow

.... then by Boot

Balloch-The Dog House

The Dog House is easy to find. If you get off the bus at the terminus, which we were supposed to do, and take a left, it is only a couple of hundred yards along the road, on a corner. Go into the bar, which is up the side street. It's a great pub.

Drymen-The Clachan Inn and The Winnock

Unlike pubs in big towns, you will have no problem finding the *'The Clachan'* or *'The Winnock'*, the bus drops you off in the square, and both pubs are in there.

Renton-The Central Bar;

It's on Main Street in Renton, you can't miss it. The bus drops you off in Main Street. If you are rich and take the train, it's a two minute walk to the pub.

Edinburgh

John: Sometimes called 'Auld Reekie', but is it old, or smelly, and does anybody care? We're looking for auld pubs. If they are a bit smelly it doesn't matter to us.

The planning was not going to be easy today. The size and layout of Edinburgh is a mystery to me. Craig had already picked out a couple of pubs that he reckoned were the oldest. Then he asked me to find my oldest pub. As is my want, I used my memory. The number of times it has dropped me in the shit is amazing. Having said that, I knew of a pub in the Grassmarket area that I had been in years ago when Kate and I were doing a wee overnight in the capital. I wasn't sure of the name, but knew exactly where it was. And it was definitely very old.

When I told Craig about my choice, he went into 'Google Earth Street View', which he told me is a feature of Google Earth, and I saw the pub I had visited, I was amazed. New technology can have its advantages.

It was a nightmare working out the buses we would have to get to take us from pub to pub. Unfortunately, it was my nightmare. God knows where we would end up? As long as it was a pub, I was not caring too much. So off we went to Edinburgh.

As usual, we have put Craig's pub first. This was not the order that we actually visited them, but it would take too long to describe how we eventually got to them at all.

Craig's 1st Pub; *The Sheep Heid Inn;* This is the pub I had most wanted to visit since we started planning this book. All the research I had compiled pointed towards The Sheep Heid Inn being the oldest pub in Edinburgh, if not Scotland. Being established in 1360, it is centuries older than any other pub we'd have come across so far.

This was my chance to beat John hands down and I was determined that this pub would be one of my choices. Not telling him anything about the place until we were actually on our way to Edinburgh certainly helped me 'acquire it' as one of mine.

Actually, finding the place proved much more difficult than conning John out of the chance to write about it. This was mainly due to John insisting on doing the navigation. I had to let him, it only seemed fair. He had prepared his usual batch of almost unreadable maps using his old printer. I've tried to tell him that for the cost of the ink it uses he could probably buy an ordnance survey map.

On this occasion we had a bit of a disagreement while travelling along on the No 44 bus to Duddingston. I told him that by my calculations we should get off at the next stop. He categorically denied this. Pointing at his crumpled, ink-stained excuse for a map he insisted that we still had another mile to go before reaching our stop. Just then the driver shouted back to us that we had reached Duddingston.

Any normal person would have given up any pretence of direction finding, not John. Like a lemming searching for a handy cliff to jump from he marched off in the wrong direction.

The oldest pub in Edinburgh, or perhaps Scotland?

Eventually we found ourselves standing outside The Sheep Heid. I had seen pictures of the place but I was still surprised at how fancy it looked. It did cross my mind that I had made a mistake choosing this pub. It just didn't look like the kind of place I would enjoy drinking in. Fortunately I was willing to give it the benefit of the doubt.

The first question asked by anyone visiting the pub for the first time is obviously, 'Where did the pub get its name?' Apparently there are at least two versions of how this name became attached to the pub.

Sheep were grazed on the royal parkland adjacent to the Duddingston area of Edinburgh. Once the sheep were killed and gutted, the carcasses were shipped to the Fleshmarket for sale to the city's residents.

The only part of the animals which was not sent for sale was the head. Locals soon discovered many ways of cooking these discarded heads, providing themselves with a continuous source of free food.

It was said that so many sheep were processed in this way at Duddingston that the skulls of the animals were used instead of cobbles on the pathways in the local area.

For many people these stories are reason enough to explain why the local pub would adopt the name of the areas' most useful commodity. As John pointed out, rather unhelpfully, it was just as well it was the sheep's head which was discarded; otherwise the pub could have had a very unfortunate name.

However there is another explanation for the name. Apparently in 1580 King James VI presented the landlord of the original pub with a very unusual gift.

The king reputedly often stopped off at this pub for a drink or two and the occasional game of skittles while travelling between Holyrood Palace and Craigmillar Castle.

James was said to be so taken with the pub that he that he presented the landlord with a very ornate snuff box, shaped in the form of a rams head.

Even in those days it paid to advertise, especially if you could boast about a bit of royal patronage. What better way to do that than name your pub in honour of the king's gift. The original snuff box has long since disappeared into a private collection, but a copy can still be seen behind the bar.

There is no definitive answer to the question of where the pub came by its unique name but, for me, the snuff box seems the most likely explanation.

With the pub history worked out we settled back to enjoy our short stay. No sooner had we plonked ourselves down on our bar stools than Kayleygh Holton, our barmaid, suggested that we should go through the back of the pub to check out the skittle lanes.

It was amazing. I had imagined that, being in a pub, it would be quite small, but it really was a full-sized affair. This particular alley was built in 1870 but skittles, in one form or another, have been played here for centuries.

Scotland's oldest bowling alley

Kayleygh insisted that we give it a go. Personally I find it easy enough to embarrass myself just going about my day, without looking for any extra opportunities to make an arse of myself. John, on the other hand actively seeks out such chances to do just that.

It is hard to imagine that a man can get to his age without having even a vague notion of how to play bowls. He launched the ball almost vertically and it barely made it to the end of the lane.

Kayleygh obviously felt some pity and tried to show him how it should be done. She was wasting her time really, as a complete lack of co-ordination and a brain befuddled by booze meant John was more likely to fall over than any of the pins.

Back through in the bar we chatted to the other two members of staff, Robin Jacobs and Colina Blair, about some of 'The Heid's more recent history.

It seems that in the distant past, the pub played host to both sides during the Covenanter's rebellion, presumably not at the same time. Bad enough they were knocking lumps out of each other on the battlefields without adding booze to the mix.

Colina, Robin and Kayleygh

Bonnie Prince Charlie was one of The Sheep Heid Inn's most prominent visitors in the mid- 1700s. Along with his Jacobite army he set up camp in and around Duddingston before giving the government forces a bit of a pasting at Prestonpans.

Fortunately things are a bit quieter nowadays in the '*Heid*', with the only battles fought there being over games of skittles and, in John's case, who was going to pay for the next round.

Despite claims that my choice of pub didn't count because it was outside the old city walls of Edinburgh, I insisted that The *Sheep's Heid Inn* be declared the winner of our search for The Auldest Boozer in Toon.

John's comments; *It's hard to argue with Craig's first choice as far as age is concerned. 1360 is a hell of a way back. But*

138

it is outside the traditional 'Walled City', I think. The pub itself is more of a lounge bar, but is beautiful inside with lots of memorabilia etc. on the walls. The two Skittle Lanes downstairs are supposedly the oldest ones in Scotland.

It's not the sort of old man's pub that we normally visit, but a good one and well worth a visit.

The Grassmarket's oldest pub

John's 1st Pub; *The White Hart Inn;* As soon as I saw the pub, I knew I was on a winner. It looks great from the outside, and the inside is brilliant. Even without all the ancient stories and tales that are on the walls and ceilings, the bar itself has a fantastic atmosphere.

The barman, Liam Falls, and the manager Susie Power told us all they could about the history of the pub, which dates back to 1516. When I told them about the *The Sheep Heid Inn* dating back to 1360, they informed me that it is outside 'The Old Edinburgh Wall', and it is also outside 'The Flodden Wall', which, I think they told me, came after The Old Edinburgh one. In their view, *The White Hart* is Edinburgh City's oldest pub. So, like every other place in Scotland, there is a debate about which pub was the oldest.

Getting the age thing out of the way, I asked how the pub got its name. Was it anything to do with Tottenham Hotspur's

139

ground in White Hart Lane. As they were both young and from Edinburgh, they had no idea what I was talking about. But they did claim to know how the pub got its name.

The story they told me (and I have my doubts) is that on a Holy Day, many hundreds of years ago, Scotland's King, I think it was David, went hunting.

This happened in the middle of winter on a day when the snow was thick on the ground. It was a Holy Day, and he shouldn't have been hunting at all. Anyway, the mythical giant White Hart beast appeared before him and was about to gore him when a flaming cross appeared between the beast's antlers.

Susie and Liam

Needless to say, the flaming cross saved the day and the pub was named after the event. I wonder if Spurs ground in London has a connection with a white legend. It has! John White, a brilliant Scots midfield player was a Spurs legend. Mind you, he was struck by lightning on a golf course and sadly died. Where were we before I started rambling. In *The White Hart* in Edinburgh

Craig and I have visited literally hundreds of pubs in our last five books, purely for research you understand. One thing we have come to realise is that there are not many that our National Bard, the great man himself Robert Burns, has not had a pint in, or a good night out with a member of the fairer sex.

The White Hart was no exception.

The story goes that near the end of his life, he spent a week in *The Hart* with Nancy Macklehose, his last lover. By the way, a week! Not bad for a guy nearing the end of the road. Well, he was moved to write what is probably the greatest love poem of all time, 'Ae Fond Kiss'. I could recite the whole poem, but you would just think I was full of shit!

Burns was not the only person who did the business in the rooms above the Inn, as it was in the old days. Burke and Hare, the famous body snatchers were seemingly regulars, who came in now and again looking for a 'carry out', probably something with a bit of body in it.

As always with old pubs, and especially in Edinburgh, there were hundreds of ghost stories, all true! But the one I am about to tell you was told to me by an old 'regular' who was sitting in the corner. I wanted to talk to him because he was a regular, and more importantly, a local. A local in a pub in the centre of Edinburgh is hard to find. The staff and everybody else in the pub came from out of town.

The only problem with Steven was that he was fairly plastered. And remember, this was early in the day. Anyway, he said this was a true story, as it had happened to him.

One day, as he was leaving the toilet, a pair of detached legs walked passed him going in the direction of the cellar, followed by the body. I asked him if he was sure he wasn't looking in the big mirror outside the toilet as if he was in the same state as he was today, it might have been him that was legless.

Edinburgh people don't have the same ability as us to laugh at themselves. Steven assured me in no uncertain terms that the story was true. Then he just got up and left the pub.

I went back and joined Craig who admitted that, unlikely as it seems, he was enjoying himself in our capital city. We were having a great time in Edinburgh.

I hate to admit it, but there are hundreds of great pubs in Edinburgh, and this is one of the very best, and a must to visit if you are in the Capital.

141

We said our goodbyes to Liam and Susie, and the ghosts of hundreds of deid people, legless or otherwise, and wandered out to find our next pub.

Craig's comments; This was a great choice on John's part. I would have a drink in there anytime, except perhaps during the Edinburgh Festival and other such celebrations. Apparently it can get very touristy in the Grassmarket during the summer months.

I thought John was going to swallow his tongue when he heard how much a round cost.

The pub manager told us that The White Hart was the oldest pub within the old city walls. This pleased John no end. I have found out since our visit that it might not be quite as old as is claimed.

It would appear that there was indeed a pub on the site where The White Hart now stands. Only the cellar ruins of that earlier pub date back to 1516.

Craig's 2nd Pub: *Ye Old Golf Tavern.* I had hoped that John would choose the Old Golf Tavern as one of his pubs, for no other reason than the fact that I don't like anything to do with golf. It is a total waste of time and money. Besides which, anytime golf is mentioned John tends to recall every upmarket golf course he has ever played. There is just no stopping him. Therefore I had every expectation of being treated to a guided tour of all the golfing memorabilia we would find in the Tavern. But if he was writing about the place, at least I wouldn't have to listen.

Getting to the place was a bit of a nightmare if it hadn't been for my smart phone we would never have found it. John was having yet another off day in the urban geography department. To be fair *The Tavern* is pretty well hidden. Only locals and well-prepared pub historians could be expected to find it easily.

It is situated on a fancy road, and overlooks Holyrood Park. We were both impressed with the area, which had a definite upmarket feel to it. However as we walked up the road towards *The Tavern* we noticed that one of the fine buildings was being converted into student accommodation. I suspect that the housing prices are about to take a nosedive in the area, while takings behind the bar of the Old Tavern are about to rocket.

From outside, *The Tavern* looks every bit as imposing as the other buildings on this road. In fact I was a bit surprised that there wasn't a uniformed flunky waiting outside to greet us at the door. Although John has obviously seen much bigger and better on his travels around the likes of Gleneagles, Royal Troon and Turnberry.

Ye Olde Golf Tavern

Up at the bar we were still a bit shell-shocked by our surroundings. John was hyperventilating by the time he had to pay for our round. I must admit I feared the worst myself. But we were pleasantly surprised by the price we were asked to pay. It seems that as soon as you get away from the main tourist areas the price drops considerably, even in swanky golf pubs.

The Tavern looks spotlessly clean and in very good order. It seems that it was completely refurbished in 2011 and they really pulled out all the stops. The quality of the decor is surprisingly high, although when you consider the matching chandeliers maybe the owners could be accused of going over the top slightly.

The ceiling itself is also highly decorated. I could be wrong but it looked like the whole thing was covered in embossed copper sheeting. You would never get away with that in a pub in Govan.

No sooner would they have finished installing it than some enterprising local part-time scrap merchant would have been loading it into the back of his transit.

Between them, Lyndsay McDonald and Jacqueline Weston, our servers, filled us in on the history of the Golf. It seems that the pub was founded in 1456, although it was previously known as *The Golf Hotel.* Back in those days there was no such thing as a clubhouse so the Inns nearest the courses benefited from the trade generated by the medieval hackers. It would be a couple of hundred years before the 19th hole was invented for Scotland's golf courses.

The Old Golf Tavern provided a meeting place for the Bruntsfield Links Society from the late 1700s until the area became too busy for the golfers, with travelling fairs and locals taking advantage of the free grazing land. Although no longer a traditional golf course the game is still played on the land just across the road from the Tavern. Bruntsfield Links is one of the very few free public golf courses left in Scotland. It is now called a short course club, but I feel sure that just means Pitch and Putt.

In fact we were told that if we fancied a round we could hire golf clubs and balls from the bar staff. As a matter of fact, we did quite fancy a quick round but, as you have probably guessed, it wasn't a round of golf we were fancying.

My only criticism of the Tavern is a very small one indeed. Even then only a small section of the pubs clientele will ever be affected by it.

144

John and Michael

The Gents toilet is downstairs and has a clear glass entrance door. While I was making good use of the facilities another customer nearly walked straight into the glass when he tried to leave. This glass door set up could very easily catch out the elderly, the short sighted and or the drunk. As far as John is concerned this is an accident waiting to happen.

It really is amazing to think that a pub, which first opened its doors in 1456, is not the auldest boozer in this toon. That honour belongs elsewhere.

John's comments; This is one of the most up-market places we have ever been in, can't even describe it as a pub. Seemingly it used to serve Edinburgh's oldest golf course. But it has gone now and they give out putters in the summer for locals to play putting. The golf might not be as glorious as in olden days, but it is a hell of a fancy pub. Got to mention that even though it is a fancy Edinburgh pub, the staff, Michael Smith, the barman, and the two girls were brilliant. It's not an old traditional pub by any means, but well worth a visit.

John's 2nd pub; *The Oz Bar;* You will not find this pub in any guide to old pubs in Edinburgh. I have no idea where this place would be included. ,

John out front in the outback bar

In my first pub, *The White Hart,* I had asked the staff if they knew where I would find another pub that could be included in this oldest pub guide. The problem was that they came up with about a hundred suggestions of places that may be the oldest, and by the time we had left and were wandering up a hill to get a bus, I had no idea of any of the names of the places they had mentioned.

I was about to give up and just do the one pub when we came to a wee corner on a hill, and *The Oz Bar* was there, right in front of us. Spontaneously, we both decided that this was going to be my next pub. If nothing else, it must be the oldest Australian Pub in the city. As most of you will know, my oldest son Campbell lives in Sydney, so I love all things Australian, especially the beer. So in we went.

Ian Pontin, the barman, and a local, made us very welcome and showed us round the bar. It is a brilliant wee place and is done up to feel like an Australian Pub, it even has a corrugated roof above the bar. It is the sort of place you would imagine in the outback of Australia. There's certainly nowhere like it in Sydney. I enjoyed a bottle of James Boags, which is one of the best beers in Australia.

Ian pulls the pints in The Oz

Ian bought the place in 1994, so by Australian history (British Australian history that is) the place is pretty old. It is a great wee Aussie bar; even the cellar is down under. One of the locals who chatted to us even bought a book. I was 'stoked'. As this was an extra pub in our schedule, and we didn't have a lot of time, too soon we had to say our g'days, get 'rugged up' and head off to our next port of call.

Craig's comments; Not exactly in its dotage, the Oz Bar first opened its doors in 1997. There were a number of factors which led us to visit this rather strange pub.

It was raining, it was freezing and it was at the bottom of a big hill we needed to climb.

It is worth a visit however, just to see the décor. Inside the converted furnishing warehouse the owner has built a fairly reasonable copy of a beach shack, complete with corrugated iron roof. I liked it.

Find oor Auld Boozers

by Bus . . . .

The No. 900 leaves Buchanan Street every 15 minutes. So no excuse to miss out on a trip to our capital city-or is there?

. . . . then by Local Bus and Boot

I have described below how to get to the pubs we visited starting out in the Princes Street area of the town. We did all the pubs in one day so we were on a variety of other buses.

The Sheep Heid Inn

Get the Nos. 44 or 44A or 124 from Princes Street going East. Get off the Bus on Willowbrae Road near Duddingstone Cross Road. It's only a short walk from there to The Causeway.

The Golf Tavern

Get the No. 45 at stop ND on the North Bridge, which is well known. Ask a local if you are lost. Mind you, finding a local in Edinburgh is not easy. Get off in Leven Street just after the King's Theatre. It's just a two minute walk from there round the corner into Wright's Houses.

The White Hart Inn

Again it's stop No. ND on The North Bridge and the bus is the same No. 45. Get off in Chambers Street. Only a few yards from there down into the Grassmarket.

The Oz Bar

And yet again it's the No. 45, again at stop No. ND on The North Bridge. Get off on King George IV Bridge and it's just round the corner and down a wee hill.

Falkirk

John: This is a wee town that is lost in the central belt of Scotland. Places like Grangemouth are better known for the big oil refineries, or whatever the big factories with the flames coming out of the chimneys do. But I like Falkirk. The centre has a good atmosphere, even if trying to get to it is not the easiest. Once, when Kate and I were driving there, we ended up in Grangemouth. Mind you, Kate was driving and I was navigating.

Apart from the pubs, there are some really fabulous, things to visit. The Falkirk Wheel and the big horses are just two, well three if you count the horses separately.

Today's visit was done on Friday the 13th of March, what could go wrong? Funnily enough, we got to Falkirk without any hitches, and that in itself is unusual. We even got off the bus before the bus station as I thought all we had to do was cut through a wee street and we would be on High Street where Waterstone's was, and I was right. We had five books to deliver, so we were killing two birds with one stone.

As usual, I only had Craig's word on what was the oldest pub in the town. I had done no background work. My idea was to ask Craig Raeside, the manager in Waterstone's for his advice on the subject. Unfortunately, it was his day off. His deputy, Symon Lloyd, was very helpful and told us he reckoned *The Wheatsheaf Inn,* just round the corner, was the oldest. Craig was listening to our conversation and claimed that was the pub he had checked out on the web, so he said he should have it as his first pub. Talk about a big wean, or as we were in Falkirk, a big Bairn!

Unfortunately, he didn't listen to the instructions about how to get there, so he had to follow me. We got lost. The pub was only about a couple of hundred yards from Waterstone's and I managed to screw up. Craig whipped out one of his magic devices and feeling very smug, got us to the pub, Craig's first of the day.

Craig's 1st Pub: *The Wheatsheaf:* You would think that by now John would have developed a sense of direction. If not, surely he would be willing to listen to those of us who are so blessed, especially if the blessed one happens to own a big fancy satnav. I have even advised him that if he really needs to get somewhere in a hurry he should decide which direction to take then turn 180° from that direction and he will soon find his chosen destination.

To cut a long story short I had to drag him kicking and screaming along to the Wheatsheaf. In the interests of accuracy I should point out that it was me who was doing all the kicking and screaming. There may also have been some swearing going on.

We were impressed by the look of the Wheatsheaf. It really wouldn't have been out of place in a very rural location. That being the case it could be said that it is slightly out of place sitting up a back street in Falkirk.

Wheatsheaf Inn, Falkirk

Inside, the place is almost picture perfect. The walls are completely clad in wood panelling and the bar takes up most of the floor area. There are three ornate fireplaces which suggest that the building has seen a fair bit of conversion over the years.

If I remember correctly there was only one telly in the bar, which is a major plus. There wasn't a lot of seating but I did spot a large comfy looking armchair.

I had made the mistake of telling John, most probably over a few drinks, that I fancied trying out some real ale on this our latest adventure. Usually he never remembers what we talk about in our sessions, but this time he took great delight in reminding me.

The Wheatsheaf prides itself on having a good selection of real ales and I expected our barman, Alastair Black, to advise me on choosing a good one. What he did say was, that if it was up to him he would always settle for a nice pint of Tennent's lager.

I admired his honesty but I asked for a pint of whatever one of the available potions tasted most like lager. He did his best but after two pints of disappointment I reverted to my beloved pint o' lager nectar!

Now that we knew we had something in common, the Tennent's Lager, I got on the chat with Alastair. He said that the pub had recently been refurbished, and I'm really glad he did as I was about to say that the wood-cladding on the walls looked so fresh that it could have been done at any time in the last 20 years, instead of back in the 18th century.

Alastair's goal is to serve great beer

We were listing our usual points for and against the ideal pub when Alastair managed to score maximum points when he informed us that since the pub didn't have a food licence there were never any kids running around the bar.

Somehow this got us onto the subject of diets and Alastair told us that he had lost three stones in weight recently. Apparently he has taken up football again. When he said that he was the goalkeeper of his team I suggested that his team couldn't be all that good if the keeper managed to lose so much weight so quickly.

As usual we asked our bar person if there were any stories he could tell us about his pub and as usual we were told we had only just missed meeting one of the pub's characters, who would have been able to tell us a few corkers.

We are either the unluckiest travellers in the country or the most easily kidded. Anyway, Alastair did manage to recall a story about one of his regulars, Robert McSorley. The poor chap died recently, but the story is still worth repeating. The old guy had been out doing his shopping and had decided to make a day of it by having a drink or two before going home. To make sure his bag of messages didn't get lost he hung it up on one of the coat hooks by the bar.

The couple of drinks he had intended having soon turned into a full blown session. Spotting an opportunity for some fun the barman and some of his customers concocted a phoney raffle. Just before he was about to leave it was announced that Robert had won the top prize. They made a great show of presenting him with his prize and applauded as he cheerily left the pub.

About an hour later the barman got a really abusive phone call from the 'prize winner' who had just discovered that he had in fact won his own messages.

I think someone did mention something about a pub ghost but I totally ignored the story as I'm fed up listening to such nonsense.

Once again we had found a really good pub and once again we made the mistake of getting too comfortable, not to mention, in John's case at least, a bit squiffy.

At this time I was convinced that my first choice was indeed the oldest pub in Falkirk. According to all my research and the sign outside the pub itself the Wheatsheaf was opened in 1797

That is not disputed but as I was to find out shortly, the exact location of the pub has been questioned.

John's comments: This is a lovely old pub and definitely worth a visit, if you can find it! While Craig was talking to the barman, I found out through talking to an old regular that 'The Tollbooth' and 'The Woodside Inn' were two pubs that were very old and worth checking out. When we were about to leave, I mentioned them to Craig. The bugger claimed 'The Woodside' was one we were planning to visit and that he had already told me about it. For a quiet life I said I remembered and that I would have The Tollbooth *as my pub. So it was back down onto High Street where the pub was very easy to find. It is behind the giant Tollbooth Steeple.*

John's 1st Pub: *The Tollbooth:* This great looking building is on the corner of Flesh Market Close, which is a bumper of a name, and Tollbooth Street, which is supposed to be the shortest street in Britain. I just hoped that my excitement about the streets would continue to the inside of the pub and its opening date.

The inside didn't let me down. This is a fine looking traditional pub with great staff. The owner, Robert Lowe, has had the place for 26 years and his loyal barmaid, Jackie Botto, has served customers for 15 years, so I was sure that between them they would know about the history of the pub, and hopefully dish some dirt on Craig's first pub.

It's John's turn to pay in the Tollbooth

They did not let me down. *The Tollbooth* has reportedly been opened since the early 1700s, they didn't manage to get an exact date, but an interesting fact Robert told me about *The*

154

Wheatsheaf is that when it originally opened, it was not on its present site, but in High Street. Does this mean it can still claim to be the oldest? I'm not sure, but in my book I was standing, if slightly unsteadily, in the oldest. At the very least, *The Tollbooth* is the oldest pub in Falkirk still on its original site. That's good enough for me.

I know Craig may say that the sign, which is attached to the building, states that it used to be called the *Gaff Tavern* and that the sign says 'Reputedly', but a sign is a sign, especially an old looking one.

Now I had cleared up the history of the opening date of the pub, I wanted to find out if it had any stories to tell, and it has a good few.

Jackie and Robert-Tollbooth veterans

Like most old pubs we have visited, there are stories of ghosts, and in most cases, drink has been involved. But *The Tollbooth* is different. Originally, it was used as a holding place for prisoners who were about to be hanged on the Gallows just outside. Stories of drinks moving about themselves and children in the room upstairs being terrified are commonplace, but the one I liked best, and the most believable, was the time the pub got an unexpected visit by the Fire Inspector who demanded to know if the fire bell was working. The second the question was out of his

155

mouth, the bell sounded for about three seconds. The inspector damn near soiled himself.

The writing high up on one of the walls sums up the people of Falkirk; it says *'Better Meddle wi the Deil than the Bairns O' Falkirk'*.

We had a great time in *The Tollbooth*. It's our type of pub and is now one of our favourites. I would class it as a real man's pub. Probably Craig's first pub, *The Wheatsheaf* would be more suited if you were unlucky enough to have the wife, or girlfriend with you.

It was with some sadness, and a bit of unsteadiness, that we said our goodbyes to Robert and Jackie and left to find Craig's next pub. By the way, as an interesting wee aside, Jackie's second name, Botto, comes from her Spanish ancestors. Thoughto you would likeo to knowo this.

Craig insisted on listening to the instructions about how to get to his next pub, and to be fair, after me turning the wrong way going out the door, he guided us there without any problems.

Craig's comments: Let me just say that I really liked the Tollbooth Inn. I liked the atmosphere of the place and the staff were great fun and very informative. However if John thinks he can claim that the Tollbooth is the oldest pub in Falkirk he can think again. The plaque on the outside wall of the pub states that there was another pub on this site before the Tollbooth Inn came into existence.

Craig's 2nd Pub: *The Woodside Inn;* John had come up with the idea of catching a local bus up to *The Woodside Inn*. His plan was for us to leave *The Tollbooth Inn* and walk round to the bus station to get said bus. You will not be stunned to hear that there was a major flaw in his strategy. I think it was Robert who pointed out that the bus station was just as far away as our next pub was. The Woodside was never in contention for the title of oldest pub, but it really is worth the effort to find it.

The pub first opened its doors in 1827. It is a very traditional pub, but brightened up by some really intricate and colourful panels of stained-glass. Apparently the panels in the two front windows are removable. At the time I failed to ask the obvious question: why?

I can only assume that at some time in the past the local peasants revolted on a regular basis. Meaning that at the first sign of trouble the publican was obliged to whip the stained glass panels out of the windows and hide them safely in the cellar. Of course there may well be a much simpler explanation.

The first thing the visitor will notice is the size of the bar. It is huge. In fact there seems to be more space behind the bar than there is on the customer side.

We go inside the Woodside Inn

This suggests to me that this pub started out as a standing bar, where men were men and chairs were unnecessary. There is a lot to be said for foot rails and oxter high bars.

We soon got chatting to the barmen George Short, the manager, and Paul Casi. They are very proud of their pub and insisted on showing us all the stained glass in the windows and doors.

John, who actually likes all those ghost stories we hear when we are out and about, was keen to find out if the Woodside had any spectral visitors. As this was one of my pubs I refused even to take notes on the subject. So if you are a fan of all things ghostly you will need to go to the pub yourself and ask the boys all about it.

One visitor I did take note of however, was a certain Mr George Best. Apparently he visited the pub many years ago. By this time the drink was having a bit of an effect on me, as it sometimes does, and I suggested that it would be more unusual to find a pub that George Best hadn't visited. I'm not sure the lads appreciated my insightful comments but they were very professional about it and didn't seem to take offence.

We swapped a few more stories and even managed to flog three books to the boys, and as usual we promptly blew the proceeds on buying a round of drinks for ourselves and our new pals.

As all serious drinkers will know it is standard practice to visit the facilities before leaving a pub. In John's case it is an imperative, as he has the bladder of a much older man. A half pint is enough to set him off on the toilet trail.

Paul and George

Perhaps we were having too much fun swapping jokes with the boys behind the bar or, maybe we are both getting a bit befuddled in our old age. Whatever the reason, we forgot to visit the smallest room before leaving. There are always consequences to your actions and todays were fairly serious.

158

Firstly by the time we arrived back at the bus station John was under a lot of pressure, quite literally. We couldn't find a toilet in the bus station and we had to go into the shopping centre to look for one. John thought he had spotted one at the top of the escalator and quickly ran forward to travel up it.

Unfortunately in his desperation to relieve the pressure he didn't notice that the escalator he was trying to go up was in fact the down one. What followed was an absolute pantomime. As he was rolling around the floor I was totally unable to help him up. I really thought I was going to hurt myself laughing. Even worse I too was in need of a visit to the loo, and there was a serious danger of something very unpleasant occurring.

It was just as well we were both a wee bit tipsy, otherwise we could well have been embarrassed by the whole affair. Obviously we did eventually find a toilet, but by that time we had managed to miss our intended bus.

For reasons neither of us really understood we ended up having to change buses at the Larbert Hospital. I took the opportunity to force-feed John lots of black coffee from the cafe in there as Kate was picking us up from the station in East Kilbride and I didn't want her to think that I had once again got her old man blootered.

John's comments; Although it doesn't claim to be the oldest pub in Falkirk, it's a brilliant one, and another that's worth a visit. There is nothing I can criticise about it. Great place and the staff were brilliant.

John; The journey home was not without its talking points. I'm sure Craig will let you know about my unfortunate incident with an escalator. We also missed our second bus and ended up having a coffee in the big hospital in Larbert. Craig's Irene was away on a wee break with her sister, so Craig thought he would be able to stay out late, but Kate invited Craig to our house for dinner, and let Irene know, so he had to come. Women have no sense of fun. Because of the time it took us to get home, we were sober. Kate was astonished. It just shows you the effect hospital coffee has on you. Mind you, by the time Craig went home, Kate was in bed and we were the worse for wear. Will we never learn? Drunk twice in the one day!

Find oor Auld Boozers

by Bus . . . .

There are a few buses that will get you there in just over an hour. The X37 and X86 are a couple that will get you there without changing buses. There are other ways that mean changing, but they can be quicker. Unless, like us, you miss the bus.

. . . . then by Boot

The Wheatsheaf Inn
It's easier to get to than my attempt. You go along the High Street, and up Baxters Wynd which is a side street almost opposite the Tollbooth. Unlike me, you can't miss it.

The Tolbooth Inn
This is even easier to find. It's behind the big Tolbooth Steeple on the High Street

The Woodside Inn
A bit more difficult to get to, but worth it. You walk up the street opposite the Bank Of Scotland on the High Street, straight through the mini roundabout and up the hill with school on your right. The pub is on the right.

Renfrew and Paisley

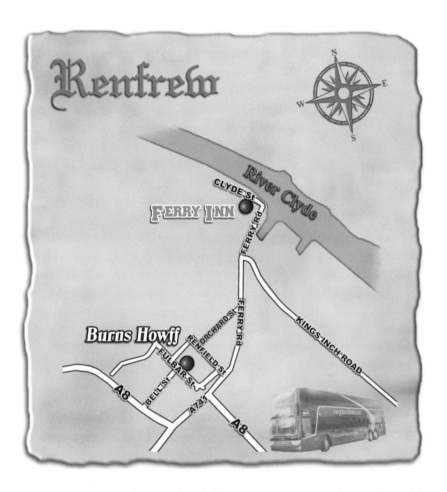

John; Renfrew and Paisley are two very underrated, and in some ways forgotten towns in Scotland. This may be because they are just outside Glasgow, but not far enough away to have their own fame. Who knows?

But they are not forgotten by the people who know what they're talking about, and by that I mean Paisley Buddies and Renfrew Ferries! Is that right?

Anyway, when I was growing up, Paisley man Gerry Rafferty was a hero of mine and one of the best song writers of all time? and that's no kidding.

There was no doubt in my mind that these two legendary towns had to be included in the book, no matter how old the pubs were. I knew of course that there were some really old pubs in the towns. In the past I have visited a couple.

Our first port of call was Renfrew. As usual, I gave Craig first pick, his choice was not a surprise. It's the one I would have chosen, if Craig ever gave me first pick.

Craig's 1st Pub (Renfrew): *The Ferry Inn;* When John came up with the idea of visiting Renfrew's oldest pubs I was less than enthusiastic. I've been to Renfrew before. In fact the oldest pub I could find in the place was one I had been to before. The Ferry Inn sits by the side of the river Clyde at the ferry crossing point between Renfrew and Yoker. The ferry, from which the Inn takes its name, runs on a half-hourly basis and it has been transporting passengers across the Clyde for over 300 years.

The Ferry Inn (or disco bar)

162

I remembered the layout of the pub from our last visit six years ago. It was a very traditional pub with lots of heavy dark wood tables and chairs. In fact the whole bar area was fairly dark gloomy. The memory of that cheered me up I began to look forward to our visit after all.

As we approached the pub I noticed that there were some guys carefully repainting the outside of the building. They were making a good job of it. The Ferry was looking great. I assumed that if the pub was being renovated so carefully on the outside, the inside would be equally well preserved. How wrong can one man be?

It was done up like the set of a bad TV gameshow. Whoever okayed the plans for this piece of pub blasphemy must have been colour blind, stone daft or probably both. Purple is not a colour that should ever be used in a Scottish pub, well not outside Edinburgh city centre at any rate. Worse still, there were pieces of quartz embedded in the surface of the bar which sparkled whenever light hit it.

John said something like, perhaps two men of our age and orientation should maybe not be seen in a place like this. I don't recall his exact words but that was the jist of it.

We were on the point of quietly slipping out of the door when our friendly barman, Norrie Mulgrew, put his head round the corner and asked us what we wanted to drink. It was too late to make a break for it, so we settled down to have a quick drink before making our excuses and heading for another pub. That this didn't happen was purely down to Norrie. His patter was so good we almost forgot about our surroundings.

It seems that a year or so back the owners discovered an area of dampness under the floor behind the bar. This shouldn't have been much of a surprise as this area of Renfrew has been prone to flooding in the past.

As an extreme example of that, Norrie told us about the time River Clyde came in to visit the pub. While they were getting the bar ready for their Hogmanay party the river overflowed its banks and the water level in the pub rose to several feet.

One of the customers, an older chap, decided to help out by doing a bit of bailing. His technique was to scoop up the water in a pail then stand on the sill and then heave it out of the open window. Unfortunately he brought more effort than skill to the task and managed to throw himself out of the window. On the plus side the high water level outside meant that he did have a fairly soft landing.

Jimmy and Carol Greaves, listening to Norrie's tales

Anyway, since they were going to have to do some major repair work it was decided that the whole bar should get a makeover. It was at this point, presumably, that the decorator got his hands on a cut-priced colour chart,-one perhaps originally meant for an upmarket Spanish bordello.

Norrie told us that the remodelling of the bar actually caused a bit of an unforeseen problem. The BBC had been using the pub as a backdrop for the comedy series 'Bob Servant: Independent', starring one of Scotland's greatest actors, Brian Cox.

When a second series was commissioned, the BBC phoned up to ask if the bar was still available, only to be told that the entire bar had been gutted. I imagine the set designers were horrified when they turned up to find a Benidorm show bar instead of a classic Scottish howff. With a lot of effort they managed to cover all the gaudy surfaces, if only temporarily.

'Taggart', the supposedly gritty Glasgow crime drama also used The Ferry's bar for a number of scenes. Our barman Norrie was in The Ferry while much of the filming was going on and managed to catch the acting bug.

He asked the director if he could play the non-speaking part of the barman in one of the scenes. The director turned him down saying, "You are not an actor". To which Norrie replied, "Well he's no a barman". He still didn't get the part.

Somebody, and it certainly wasn't me, asked if the pub had a ghost. Norrie was just about to launch into what would probably, if you believe in all that nonsense, have been a fascinating story about the wandering spirit which haunted the pub when I stopped him, saying, "Unless this ghost does tricks, like juggling or playing a musical instrument I don't want to hear about it".

It is claimed that the Ferry first opened its doors in 1703, which would certainly make it the oldest pub in the area. Since that time there have been a series of additions and modifications to the building. The first of the major alterations was completed in 1829, and many people assume that this date refers to the age of the pub. Indeed that date is engraved on the outside wall of the building and appears on a plaque above the fireplace in the bar.

I very much doubt if there will be a plaque going up to commemorate this latest upgrade of the pub.

We were told that The Ferry Inn may well be about to change hands. The rumour is that the owners of the River Ferry have made an offer for the pub.

One of the guys who had been painting the outside of the building said he hoped they would be better at running a pub than they were at running the ferry.

It seems that not long after the new ferry was introduced it ran out of fuel midstream. The ferry ended up down the river at

Govan. Due to the tidal nature of the river it had to stay there for twelve hours.

No mention was made of the unfortunate passengers but I imagine some of them had a lot of explaining to do to their partners. Trying to sell the story that it took you twelve hours to cross a fifty yard stretch of water would take some doing.

We enjoyed our stay in *The Ferry Inn* and asked Norrie to give us a call when the new owners came to their senses and chucked out all that purple nonsense.

John's comments: There's no real doubt in my mind that Craig may have come up with the oldest pub, and a good one at that. My only grievance is that the bar has been done up to look like the inside of a brothel. It's all purple, sparkles and chrome bar stools. I felt it was up to me to find the oldest pub in Renfrew that didn't look like a brothel. When I asked the barman if The Ferry *had any competitors who claimed to be the oldest, he said that* The Wheatsheaf *had claimed to be the oldest, but that it had changed into a Bistro Restaurant. I wasn't sure what that meant, but it isn't a pub, I think. I was starting to worry that there wasn't another pub in Renfrew to challenge* The Ferry.

But help was at hand. One of the guys who was taking a break from painting the outside of the pub (hopefully not purple) heard me asking and told me I should try The Burns Howff, *which is a really old pub. He said we would have no problem finding it as it is just behind the Town Hall Tower, a famous Renfrew landmark. So that's where I told Craig we were heading next.*

John's 1st Pub (Renfrew): *The Burn's Howff.* We wandered up the street, but before we went into *The Howff,* we were confronted by the sight of two guys holding big dogs on leads shouting at each other. One of them was trying to belt his opponent with the end of his dog's lead. A crowd was gathering and youngsters with camera phones were taking advantage of a chance to be on 'you-tube', or whatever it's called.

166

Now I know that people can be very protective over their dogs, but this was getting out of hand. Craig was desperately trying, without success, to find his camera, which was in his haversack, which, by the way, I was carrying.

While these two guys were acting like animals, the two dogs were as happy as Larry, probably asking each other if they would like a lick of their arse. Humans could learn a lot from our canine friends. Although the arse licking is going a bit far.

Burns Howff, Renfrew

Anyway, we got fed up and went into *The Burn's Howff*. My first impressions were very good. It is a traditional man's pub that still retains the original features that old guys like Craig and I appreciate. The barmaid, Gillian McGivern, was very helpful and tried to answer our questions, but said that the owner Gayle Brown would be the best person to ask, and she would be in in the evening. As we would both be sound asleep by then, I said we

167

would make do with her and the locals at the bar to get any information we could.

We did find out that *The Howff*, although not the oldest by date, it is the second oldest. But it is the oldest Pub in Renfrew that doesn't look like a brothel, so I'm going to claim it as the rightful oldest pub in Renfrew.

This is definitely one of the friendliest pubs we have visited, and one in which the staff and regulars go out of their way to help some of the less fortunate in the area. This came to my notice when I saw an old guy at the end of the bar having his dinner. As I had found out that the pub doesn't do food, I asked Gillian what was the score. Digger, I think his name was, is not in the best of health and has trouble looking after himself, so the bar staff organise food for him and help him to and from his home. This is a great thing to do as it helps the old guy know he is still part of the community, and not just stuck in some old folks' home.

Gillian our barmaid brings tae me a pint o lager

Having said that, good deeds like this can lead to some funny incidents. One night an old regular called Hector had had a skinful and Gayle, instead of just throwing him out as other publicans might have done, drove him home. As he left her car and was staggering the last few steps to his close, he was hustled into a police van. Gayle feared for the worse, but half an hour later Hector came back into the bar asking for more drink. Gayle found out eventually that the Policeman was Hector's granddaughter's husband, who didn't want Hector trying to get up the stairs by himself. A great story, even if I say so myself!

The *Howff* would be a great place to have as a local. As well as the bar, there's a nice lounge with some brilliant old paintings. The bar itself has a great painting of Tam O' Shanter in full flight. There is other Burns memorabilia on the walls, and I should have asked about the association between Robert Burns and *The Howff*. Mind you, Burns has drunk, slept, or at least spent time in bed in about half the pubs we have visited in Scotland. A hell of a man! This is a brilliant wee bar tucked away, but easy to find, just behind the Town Hall Tower.

After another round, we said our goodbyes to Gillian and the locals, made our way back up to the main street for our bus to Paisley.

Craig's comments: I feared the worst when we landed in Renfrew. Watching two Jakies squaring up to each other on the main street didn't bode well. Then having to search for a back street pub didn't sound like a sensible idea.

Fortunately The Burn's Howff *turned out to be a great wee pub. It obviously isn't the oldest pub in town but we enjoyed our visit.*

Craig's 1nd Pub (Paisley): *The Bull Inn;* The Bull Inn on New Street Paisley was suggested to me as the best prospect for the title 'Auldest Boozer in Toon'. Unfortunately the 'suggestee' was my drinking partner and competitor, John.

It serves me right for listening to him. But in my defence, I had been suffering, silently, from a bad cold and probably wasn't at the top of my game.

As soon as I saw the outside of the pub I began to suspect that I had been set up. Right up above the front door in large letters

I saw it written, 'established 1901. Knowing the good folk of Paisley have never been averse to the odd drink or two I was fairly certain that there would be pubs out there older than The Bull Inn.

Obviously I didn't let this put me off wandering into the pub for a beer or two.

The Bull Inn, Paisley

Even from the outside I was sure it would be a decent pub, but I was completely unprepared for what it looked like inside. It was amazing. If you have ever visited the Glasgow School of Art, before it went on fire obviously, you would notice a great resemblance. It is all dark wood, elegant lighting and stained glass.

After ordering our drinks I told Graeme Leggate, our barman, that I was very impressed by his pub's décor. He told us that it had all been designed by a student of Charles Rennie Mackintosh, the architect/designer of Glasgow School of Art. The entire bar structure is protected by a National Heritage listing.

I have to admit to a certain amount of smugness when I heard this. It was hard to tell if John was impressed by my knowledge of architecture as he often grinds his teeth and mumbles when he talks to me.

Graeme told us that the Bull does a good trade in real ale and is a supporter of Paisley's Beer Festival. I have found that it makes life a lot easier if I pretend to be interested when people talk about real ale as they tend to get a bit huffy when I mock it as a total waste of time.

The layout of this pub is really quite unusual. It is a much larger pub than you would imagine, being three or four times as long as it is broad. It seems that the building which now houses the pub was once a carriers and livery.

There are glass booths or snugs at the far end of the bar and these can be booked for private parties.

We were told that in the dim and distant past these booths had frosted glass fitted. Legend has it that ladies plying their trade in the world's oldest profession were allowed to conduct their business in these booths.

Graeme, manager of the Bull

If true, it would seem that Paisley Town Council was a particularly open-minded organisation. Having had dealings with town councils I can state without fear of contradiction that Scottish councils are not known for their liberal views.

Although it must be said that they do seem to like the odd expenses-paid, fact-finding junket, so you just never know.

Although we were the only customers in this huge bar I noticed that there were small coal fires burning away in each booth. When we had first come in we had been complaining about the weather. Snow and sleet are never really welcome but especially not at the end of April. Anyway, Graeme had suggested that we go and sit in one of the booths until we warmed up a bit. At the time I thought he was just trying to get rid of us when in fact he was doing a grand job of looking after his customers.

While we were chatting away about places we have visited on our travels Graeme mentioned a pub in Hamilton. It turns out that his dad owned it. That got John's attention. It also steered the conversation away from the business in hand and onto the subject of John's favourite pubs in Hamilton.

I decided to wander off to take some pictures as there are an awful lot of pubs in Hamilton and he has been in them all. By the time I got back to the bar the conversation had moved onto movies.

It seems that the interior of *The Bull Inn* features in the 2008 Scottish film, 'Stone of Destiny'. After another beer we decided it was time to fulfil our own destiny and move on to our second historical Paisley pub.

On every web site I looked at it was claimed that The Bull Inn was the oldest pub in Paisley. Normally I would be only too glad to accept that as fact but, what we found round in Smithfield Road brought that into question.

John's comments: No arguments from me here about The Bull *being one of the best looking bars I have ever been in. But is it the oldest. A local who came in covered in snow, spoke to me when he had heated up and was very interested in our quest. The old pubs that is, not the getting pissed each trip. He told me, in a quiet voice, that there was another pub in Paisley that he thought may be older. In a secretive voice, he let me know it was called* Old Swan, *and was just a five minute walk away. I thanked him and said we would head over to it if the snow stopped.*

Even if we find out that The Bull *is not the oldest, I must agree with Craig's comments about the pub. It is a fantastic place, and a must to visit.*

As a wee footnote, an interesting fact I found out from Graeme is that his dad Jim owns The Victoria Bar, *which, in my opinion, is the best pub in Hamilton.*

John's 1st Pub (Paisley); *The Old Swan;* This is not as fancy a pub as Craig's *Bull,* but it's a great looking pub inside and out. We went in in a rush as it was starting to snow again, and this was near the end of April. No wonder so many people spend their time in pubs in Scotland. The weather is awful.

An old buzzard outside the Old Swan, Paisley

The bar was very busy for a Monday afternoon, and the barmaid Alison Campbell told me that the pub is always busy. There seems to be something happening all the time. Pub quizzes, live bands, and karaoke nights are regular events, as well as raising money for charity, for which the pub is rightly famous.

Unfortunately, Alison was just in helping out for the owner Jacquoline McCaig, who would be in later. Fortunately, there were a great crowd of locals in who told us all about the history of the pub, and their own history of drinking in the place. One of them, John Smith, who is in his 80's, although it's hard to believe it looking at him, said he had drunk in the *Old Swan* since he was 17. That's a hell of a lot of pints. Jim, and his drinking partners, Ian Campbell and Patsy Sheenan showed us a lovely round Mosaic Tiled floor which featured a Swan. Now the surprising thing is that the date, which was in the pattern, was 1898. Now if my memory is correct, I think this makes the *Old Swan* older than *The Bull* by about three years.

Another feature of the bar I liked was that there were two chandeliers which were terrific looking and gave the place a bit of class. This is a brilliant bar which is very friendly and a lovely way to spend an hour or so if the wife is shopping in Paisley.

Ian, Patsy and John enjoy necking a few in The Swan

As to which of the two bars in Paisley is the oldest, it's a bit of a toss-up, but visit them both, you won't be disappointed.

Craig's comments: I knew I was in trouble when I first clapped eyes on this pub. It looks as if it should be the oldest pub in Paisley. Even then I wouldn't admit it though. It was only when I spotted the swan mosaic on the floor of the pub that I had to concede.

There for everyone to see was the date the pub was built: 1898. Finding it was so annoying that I needed a drink. Fortunately we were standing in a really fine pub so that worked out just fine.

John: Homeward bound. We decided that since it was freezing and snowing, we would just dive into Paisley Gilmour Street and get the train to the Central Station and then the EK train home. It's a lot quicker, warmer, and only costs a couple of quid with the bus pass. We were not sure about the train times, so for no good reason, we popped into a pub next to the *Old Swan.* It was called *The Tiles,* and we enjoyed a quick one while asking about train times, which were one every 10 minutes.

So ended our adventures in Renfrew and Paisley.

Find oor Auld Boozers

by Bus . . . .

No problem for the Bus Pass holder, or you youngsters who pay.
The X23 will take you from Glasgow to Renfrew
The 26 goes from Renfrew to Paisley.
The 9 will take you from Paisley to Glasgow
Now I know it's not in the spirit of our travels, but because Paisley is less than 10 miles from Glasgow, the train is dead cheap for the pensioners, only about 90p single (£1.30 return) at time of writing. On a hellish wet and windy day, the train will drop you off at Paisley Gilmour Street. Of course, it will do the same thing on a dry sunny day.

. . . . then by Boot

The Ferry Inn (Renfrew)
Turn right at the Town Hall and it's a five minute walk down to the Clyde. The pub's right at the ferry.

Burns Howff (Renfrew)
It's in Fulbar Street which is right behind the Town Hall Tower.

Bull Inn (Paisley)
Get off the bus outside the Town Hall, carry on up the pedestrian part of High Street, and it's first on the left into New Street.

The Old Swann (Paisley)
From the Town Hall, cross the road and it's the first street on your left, Smithhills Street.

Kilmarnock

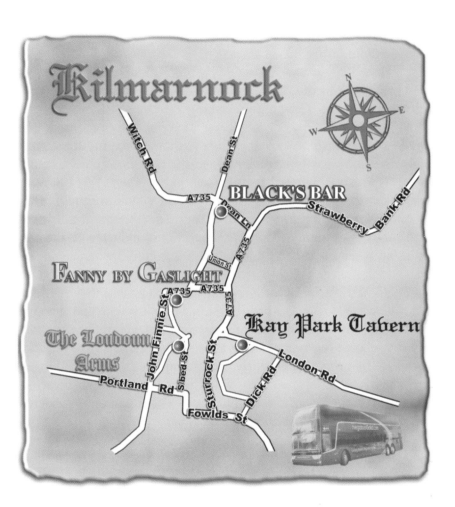

John: Kilmarnock is Ayrshire's biggest town and was famous for whisky, but no more, for the bottling plant is now shut, I think. But there are many other things Kilmarnock is famous for. What, I've no idea. But as this chapter unfolds, we will find where the good old pubs are, well hopefully we will. We'll definitely find some pubs!

Because Craig has lived and worked in Kilmarnock in his distant past, he knew all the pubs, so I left him in charge of where we would go.

It was a glorious spring day when we made our way down to Ayrshire. We got off the bus the stop before the Bus Station, right outside Craig's first choice of pub.

Craig's 1st pub: *Black's Bar;* When we started out on this book I more or less insisted that I should get the really old pubs to write about. It was really quite easy to get John to agree to this I have to say. Like anything else I want to slip past him I just wait until he is on his fourth or fifth drink before I 'suggest' whatever it is I want. He usually goes along with these suggestions, and even on the odd occasion when he doesn't I just tell him that he did when he sobers up.

It's a trick I learned from experience over the years. On today's outing however I didn't take my usual stance and demand that I get to write about the *Loudon Arms* or *Fanny by Gaslight.* My first choice for today was *Black's Bar.* Even a novice, or John, could see that *Black's* is a fairly modern pub in the scale of things.

My reason for choosing it was purely personal. I have lost count of the number of times I have passed this pub and wondered what it was like on the inside. Today was the day that at last I was to find out.

Black's Bar stands on the corner of Dean Lane and Wellington Street.

Many years ago Dean Lane was the main road up to Glasgow and whether on the bus or in the car this pub always featured as a meeting place. Even now the route of the X 16 from East Kilbride passes by *Black's* on its journey to and from Ayr.

Back in my younger days, while at school in Kilmarnock, I was made very aware that the area around the pub was not one for the fainthearted. I think they may actually have coined the phrase 'knuckle draggers' with this particular area in mind. Despite this I always quite fancied going in there and, with me in charge of the planning I made sure that *Black's* was our first port of call.

As soon as we got through the door I knew that the wait had been worth it. Even if I had managed to visit the pub all those years ago I doubt very much if the decor would have been much different. This was real time-warp stuff today, in the best possible way.

Black's Bar-much better than it looks!

I knew we were onto a good thing when the customers wished us a good morning as soon as we got through the door. As it was just after 11.30 am there were only about four or five other customers in the place. On a busy Saturday night I would imagine that there is enough room in the bar for about 40 or 50 customers.

Up at the bar we met the owner of *Black's*, Tony Kennedy, and within a few minutes we were chatting away about pubs in general and *Black's Bar* in particular. Tony has owned the pub for years and is only the third owner. The pub first opened its doors in 1939 and was purpose-built for the job.

Except for a few minor modifications very little has been done to the structure and decor of the place. For all the size of the pub the actual bar has to be the thinnest I have ever seen. It could only be about a foot wide, just enough room for a couple of pint glasses.

There is a definite football feel to the place with more than a hint of support for a certain Glasgow team. If I was to say that Andy Goram has been known to pop in there now and again I think you'll be able to guess to which particular Glasgow team I am referring. Tony himself is a former professional football player, having played for Queen of the South and Kilmarnock.

We chatted for a while about places I used to know in Kilmarnock. I went to school there and also worked in the town for a few years after that. It turns out that just about everything I remembered about the place had either, changed, closed or been knocked down.

Tony, great barman, smooth beer, rough pub

Just for a bit of nostalgia I ordered a pint of Tartan Special. John nearly fell off his stool at this point. But I couldn't be sure whether he was just shocked by my change of beverage, or his dizzy spells had returned.

We asked Tony and some of his customers if they could tell us where we could find the oldest pub in Kilmarnock. Not surprisingly that lead to a fairly boisterous discussion. It would seem that a number of pubs which I used to know around Kilmarnock Cross had, like the Cross itself been bulldozed years ago.

Once we had finished our trip down memory lane two pubs were mentioned which actually fitted in with our needs: they were old and they still existed. *The Kay Park Tavern* and *The Loudon Arms* went to the top of our list of pubs to be visited.

With that business concluded we settled back to enjoy your drinks and soak up the patter. While we were doing this somebody came into the pub with the oddest wee dog I have seen in ages. It looked like a miniature albino bulldog, and it seemed to be a bit hyperactive. John who could hardly be described as an animal lover asked Tony what kind of dog it was. He replied "It's a Sooner". What exactly is a Sooner we both asked?

"It would sooner pish in here than go outside" he told us. That's Kilmarnock humour for you.

John's comments: The pub opened in 1939, so Craig was a bit down as it's not even close to being the oldest in Kilmarnock, but it is a brilliant pub and we were made very welcome. One of the more depressing things we learned in the pub was that there are a huge number that are shut. Every time Craig mentioned the name of an old pub he was planning to visit, he was told it was shut. Craig said this was no problem as he knew all the old pubs in Kilmarnock. What worried me was that he was probably barred from most of them! Our planning would have to be done on the hoof. Black's is just a wee walk from the Bus Station and well worth a visit. More of a man's pub than one to take the wife. I'm saying this as a compliment, not a complaint.

John's 1ˢᵗ pub: *Fanny by Gaslight;* I was sure I was on to a winner with the oldest pub when we walked up to the entrance. It is a fantastic looking place from the outside, and I noticed the sign stating it was opened in 1846.

The inside of the pub is one of the best I have ever seen. The decoration is all Victorian style, I think. The bar itself has a three-tier gantry. This is a truly magnificent structure. I learned from Lawrie Headley, the owner, that the word gantry means a shelf that holds barrels. This gantry looked as if it would have no problem holding a few barrels. I didn't know that, or a lot of other things for that matter.

The name says it all!

The pub is of special historic interest and Lawie gave me a leaflet detailing the history. To be honest, there is too much detail to even try and include it in a chapter of a book like this, but the pub is a must to visit.

Lawrie, along with Alana Reid and Emma McGinn, the barmaids, were great company and made us very welcome. Craig was delighted when he discovered that Lawrie was into junior football in Ayrshire, but was less than impressed when he found out that he had been the chairman of Hurlford, one of Craig's Auchinleck Talbot's deadly enemies, and opposition for the up and coming Scottish Junior Cup semi-final. Having said that, every junior team in Scotland, and in particular Ayrshire, are 'The Bot's' enemy. By the way, 'The Bot', is Auchinleck Talbot's attempt at a Knickname. The hint's in the last three letters of the name!

Lawrie, Alana and Emma

Craig's attempts at abusing the good people of Hurlford were shot down by Lawrie when he told us the true story of a murder that occurred in Auchinleck. Seemingly, the Police took a DNA sample and have 3000 suspects. I can't repeat Craig's reply.

All too soon it was time to leave this cathedral type pub. This is one of Kilmarnock's treasures and should be put on your list of things to see in Ayrshire.

Craig's comments: Although it has been modernized in recent times it is still a great drinking-man's pub.
I got the impression that the clientele is a bit on the younger side later on in the night, but it suited me just fine for a wee afternoon binge.

Craig's 2nd pub: *The Kay Park Tavern* is yet another pub I have often walked past but never entered. It is on London Road near the Grand Hall, one of Kilmarnock's best-known dancing venues of yesteryear. More importantly it's only a few minutes' walk from the bus station.

We strolled into the Tavern and ordered our drinks and almost immediately got into conversation with some of the blokes at the bar. As soon as I asked about the age of the pub everyone at the bar got involved.

It had been very hard getting any information about Kilmarnock's pubs from the Internet. We find that it is sometimes helpful to get an independent opinion on certain parts of our investigations, as very often the people we are talking to can be chemically distracted. I did manage to get a list of pub names but no other details. We needed to find out if some of the names could be in the reckoning as the oldest pubs in town.

'A real man's pub'

The Tudor Inn certainly looked like a fairly ancient building when I saw a picture of it on my computer, but one of the lads told me that it had shut a couple of years ago. Likewise, The Crown, another pub further down Tichfield Street. My last option was The Hunting Lodge but sadly it too had closed its doors quite recently.

I was beginning to think that if we waited long enough in any pub we did find open not only would it be the oldest pub but it was quite likely it would be the only one.

As usual I asked some of the boys at the bar if they had any tales to tell us about their pub but apart from slagging each other off they failed come up with any stories of note. However the barman, William Warnock, did say it was a pity that T*he Auld Hoose* was no longer open. It seems that a while ago the circus came to Killie town and to advertise the show they had a parade up the main street. For some reason the elephant leading the parade managed to find its way into T*he Auld Hoose*. Apparently a national newspaper managed to capture a photograph of an African elephant enjoying a pint of India Pale Ale up at the bar.

While I was taking pictures around the bar one of the guys pointed at a selection of photographs on a noticeboard by the door. He said they called it the Deid Wa'. Apparently you only get your mug shot up there when you pass on. Among the photos of former pub regulars and sporting heroes I noticed a picture of Davie Cooper pinned up next to one of Jimmy Johnstone.

Tam Murphy, Derek Barclay, Jim Chrichten, Jim Crawford, Sam Craig and William Warnock

One of the drinkers we talked to seemed to be getting more than his fair share of abuse from the others. It seems that he has two strikes against him in the popularity stakes. He is a local councillor which, in my opinion, means he deserves all he gets, but far worse than that, he is originally from Ayr.

As rivalries go, the Kilmarnock/Ayr rivalry makes any bad blood between Rangers and Celtic fans seem like a minor disagreement about etiquette. Actually I would say that things had improved greatly in the intervening years since I was around in Kilmarnock. Back then if you had found an Ayr man in your pub it is quite feasible that a quantity of tar and feathers would have been required to resolve the situation.

It seems that the Kay Tavern was formerly a coaching station, which would suggest a date somewhere in the 1700s. This would put the Kay Park in the frame for being the oldest pub. But we could find no actual evidence to back this up. Although our barman did say the pub owner had checked the official records kept in Kilmarnock's main library, the Dick Institute, and he was convinced that his pub was indeed of that vintage.

Once again the name of *The Loudon Arms* came up in conversation and we decided that it would have to be investigated, even though I remember being in that pub before and was in no real hurry to return to it.

Fanny by Gaslight was also mentioned as being one of Kilmarnock's older booze emporiums. Using my vast knowledge of the town I confidently stated that there had been no pub on that site back in the 70s.

One of the boys shot me down straight away. He asked me if I had ever heard of *The Fifty Waistcoats*. Far too late to retain even a shred of credibility, I remembered that not only had that been the former name of Fanny's but that I had spent many a happy Saturday afternoon in the place. I immediately decided to resign my position as pub historian.

This seemed like the ideal moment to move on to our next pub.

186

John's comment's: This was a real old and run down looking pub from the outside. The inside, and the locals were a perfect match for the outside. Having said that, it is a great bar, and a must to visit if you have a wee bit of time to kill till your next bus. The barman and the team of locals you see in the picture were all great company. It may also be the oldest pub that is still open in the town. Another fine pub for a pint and some good chat.

John's 2nd Pub: *The Loudon Arms;* Unlike my first pub, this one is not much to look at from the outside. But this does not matter if it is the type of pub we like inside. If it is the oldest in town, it will be a bonus for me. Before we went in, I read a plaque beside the pub giving details of the bridge which is attached to it. I decided that when we built up the nerve to go in, I would try and find out more of the history of the bridge. This book may be about old pubs, but if the attached bridge has a history, we should know about it.

This pub might benefit from some cafe style seating outside- or maybe not?

Inside, the pub is nothing to write home about. I can't think of anything, good or bad, to say about it. But again, this does not matter a jot if the drink, and the company are good, and they were.

My first question to the barman, Dale Henderson, was how old the pub was. 'Very', was his reply. 'Good enough for me', I answered. Dale turned out to be a great guy and filled us in with some of the history of the place. When I asked him about the old bridge attached to the pub, he told an interesting tale. Seemingly, The Old Town Bridge, attached to the pub, was built in 1762, and a few years later a new bridge was built just along from it. In the old days, there was a tunnel between the bridges known as 'The Hole in the Wa', and it was used as a jail to hold 'The Covenanters' before they would be hanged, burned, or killed in some other more imaginative way. Now, I have my doubts about the story, and what it has to do with the book. I have no idea, but these historical stories are important to pass down to future generations, even if my interpretation is not completely accurate. Where was I? Yes, *The Loudon*.

Dale looks after the crowd'n the Loud'n

Dale then told me another interesting fact that I feel should be included. *The Loudon* was the oldest pub in Kilmarnock not to

188

have a Ladies Toilet. Now that's the sort of information we are interested in.

It's a difficult wee pub to find, hidden up a side street behind the bus station, and maybe it's best to be hidden away from the tourist. But for real hard men like Craig and me, it's worth a visit. Definitely don't take the wife.

Craig's comments; *Despite its location, the look of the place and the fact that I was feart to go in, I really quite enjoyed our short visit to* The Loudon Arms.

One look at the picture I took of the outside of this pub might well be enough to scare off potential customers. Next to a tattoo parlour and beside a rubbish dump, even a really good pub could appear less than picturesque. The Loudon *had no chance!*

John; After visiting four pubs, we still managed to get an earlier bus than planned. The sun was shining when we got off in EK, so it was into *The Lum* for a de-briefing before heading home. Another great day out.

Find oor Auld Boozers

by Bus . . . .

The X76 from Buchanan Street Bus Station will take you all the way to the Kilmarnock Bus Station.

. . . . then by Boot

Black's Bar
Get off the bus from Glasgow at the stop before the Bus Station, you will see the pub right on the corner, you can't miss it.

Fanny by Gaslight
It's on West George Street, opposite the train station. It's about a five minute walk from the bus station.

Kay Park Tavern
From the bus station, go out at the side the buses come in at, cross the road and go up the hill at the left hand side of the old town hall, I think it is. You'll find it on the right hand side.

The Loudon
Go out the back of the bus station and through the shopping mall. You'll come out in a wee square. Just cross it and it's first left, the pubs on the left just before the Old Bridge.

Dunfermline

John; The journey to Dunfermline is one we have done many times, either to deliver books to the local Waterstones, or to review pubs for one of our earlier books. Today's trip was incident free, meaning I had not fouled up on the timetable stakes. The No. 18 into Glasgow and the X26 Leven service had us in Dunfermline around noon.

Normally, Craig wants to report on the first pub we visit; this is because he has checked out the web and found which pub is reckoned to be the oldest. When we were planning today's trip, he said that I could take the first pub. Initially I was suspicious of his motives for this act of kindness, but recently I have turned the tables on him by finding out that what the web advises as the oldest pub is not always the way it turns out. Nevertheless, I thanked him for his kindness and that evening I got the wife (Kate) to check out on her high tech machine what was the oldest pub in Dunfermline.

She informed me that there was no doubt on the web that the oldest pub in Dunfermline was called *The Old Inn*. This seemed a bit daft to me. If this was the first pub to be opened in Dunfermline, I would have thought it would have been called The First Inn, or something like that.

With this information tucked away in my memory (I wrote the name down), we got off the bus in the station, wandered along the High Street, turned left into the Kirkgate and there it was; my pub in Dunfermline.

John's 1st Pub; *The Old Inn;* As soon as we went into the pub, I was sure that this was a really old drinking den. The decoration and memorabilia inside and outside the pub reeked of ancient times. It is right next to Dunfermline Abbey which has a graveyard and other ancient things. Among other historical facts, the sign outside tells you that this was the first Coaching Inn of its kind in the whole of Scotland and dates back to the 1600s.

As is my norm, I will not bore you with lots of historical information that is fairly dry and can be found in the many books that have been written on the subject. I want to tell you local, interesting things, about the place.

The manager, Calum Miller, and the barmaids Chloe Veitch and Joanna James, were great company and answered all my questions, as well as telling some interesting and some sad tales about the pub.

Craig does not believe in stories of pubs that are haunted, and to his great annoyance, this one is a bumper. Clairvoyants have visited the pub and announced that it is haunted by a young boy with blond hair. Chloe confirmed the story by telling us that quite often when she opens the pubs kitchen door, strands of blond hair will fall over her face. Craig's comment about using more hair spray was not well-received. If that was not enough for Craig, Joanna recalled the time when she was coming up the stairs from the Pool Room, which was hosting a party, and a balloon followed her up the stairs through the bar and into the ladies toilet. I said that this is not unusual as you are a good looking girl and the balloon probably had a few beers in him. 'No, she replied, it was a real blow-up balloon'.

The Old Inn (the name says it all)

Apart from its longevity and ghosts, other amazing facts we learned about the pub are that the gantry is the original one, and that the cellar is one of only two in Britain that still has a working Water Pump. This is still used for raising goods from the Cellar up to the Bar. Amazing!

The Old Inn was the oldest Coaching Inn in Scotland and ferried passengers to Leith to catch steamers heading all over the world. Its most famous coach was called 'The Fly' and was pulled by very fast horses. On a sad note, one night there was a terrible storm in Dunfermline, and the tower which stood next to the pub, or coaching inn as it was then, collapsed on top of the stables and the horses were all killed. A sobering story from the past.

The bar itself is a brilliant one. The decoration and gantry are all ancient and the whole place is very atmospheric, altogether a great bar with brilliant staff-all you need.

Another interesting fact is that this is the premises in which the legendary Dunfermline Athletic were founded. Many great players, too many to mention, played for this famous club, and their photographs adorn the walls, bringing back memories of the past when Scotland produced a conveyor belt of world-class players.

Calum, Chloe and Joanna

I cannot finish my story of the oldest pub in Dunfermline without telling you about the 'Riddle Window', for which the pub is justifiably famous.

In the year 1704, a Riddle was inscribed in one of the windows of the pub. This window became known the world over as 'The Riddle Window', a good name for it. Anyway, in 1857, changes were made to the pub and the window was removed and some time later was destroyed. Nobody knows who did this hellish deed. In fact, nobody is sure who inscribed the Riddle in the window in the first place. Luckily, the Riddle was copied and is hanging on the pub wall.

Calum told me that almost nobody has worked out the answer to the Riddle, although he claimed to know. He told me that if anybody can work out the answer, he, or she, or the ghost gets a free pint. So here it is!

To five and five add fifty-five
The first of letters add
Twil name a thing, T'would please a King
and make a wise man mad.

Craig and I have decided that if any of our readers work out the correct answer and send it to us written on a fiver, we will send you a free copy of the book, or any of our other books. We assume if you are replying to us then you have read this one. You will also get a free drink at the pub, which is well worth the visit. You will find directions to the pub at the end of this chapter.

So ended our visit to what is definitely Dunfermline's oldest pub, or is it? Craig had a sly look on his face when we left. Did he find out about another pub from Mitch, a local worthy we were talking too, or was it just that he was half cut already. Only time and the next pub would answer that question.

Craig's Comments; *The Old Inn is a great looking pub, and there is no denying that it is the oldest pub in town.*

Despite the inevitable ghost story I enjoyed our visit.

Incidentally, I too have witnessed that balloon following phenomenon. I once saw 5,000 balloons following 11 other balloons. Being a Partick Thistle supporter can't be easy. Just ask John.

Craig's 1ˢᵗ Pub; *Raffles Sports Bar;* Since I already knew that The Old Inn was the oldest pub in Dunfermline I felt quite happy leaving it to John. We had already visited it a couple of years ago. Of course John thought I was up to something by not demanding first choice of venue and I was happy about that as well. I like to keep him guessing.

My real plan was simply to ask whoever we happened to meet in our first stop if they happened to know of any really old pubs in the town. Sometimes the simplest plans are the best plans. Then again sometimes they are pish.

One of our fellow imbibers in The Old Inn told me that a pub with the unlikely name of 'SOMEWHERE ELSE' was a good age and well worth a visit. The fact that he split his drinking time between these two pubs was enough to convince me that his suggestion had to be a decent little boozer.

Either there are two pubs with the same names, or my new pal must have been seriously under the weather when I spoke to him.

We made our way up the road, following the precise directions we had been given. We only got lost twice, which is not bad going for us.

As it turned, out all of that navigation was completely wasted. I opened the door and for a moment I was rendered speechless. I'm the first to admit that this doesn't happen very often, especially after a couple of relaxing brews. But the sight before my eyes was hard to take in.

This place wasn't really a pub. It looked like the kind of place where the Woman's Institute would gather for a cup of tea and little bit of vicious gossiping. True there was a small bar at the back of the room, but it just didn't look right.

There was no way we could enjoy a drink in that place. Fortunately John came to my rescue. He pretended to look around the place as if he was looking for someone. "Do you see him?" he asked in a loud stage whisper. I caught on to what he was up to and said that I couldn't see him.

With that we slowly reversed out of the pub before scuttling along the street as fast as we could manage.

We were still in mid scuttle when I noticed *Raffles*. I had seen a reference to this pub on the net, but I didn't know anything about it. But I guessed from the ancient looking windows that the pub would be really quite old as well.

It's funny how things never turn out the way you imagine they will. It is also rather funny how I never seem to learn that lesson.

Raffles, a real gem of a pub

Raffles is a long narrow traditional pub. It was quite busy but John managed to find enough room for us both to get an elbow onto the bar. We were right in the middle which proved to be an excellent position. Almost as soon as we got there the barmaid spotted us and came straight over. Prompt service tends to impress us and we settled back to enjoy our stay.

Within a couple of minutes we found ourselves in conversation with one of the pubs larger than life characters. Brian Keenan is one of those guys who will talk to anyone. Every pub should have one.

To be honest it usually takes a little while for pub customers to warm to our company. It might be the West Coast accents or, more likely the rather suspect humour and loud voices. None of these seemed to bother Brian.

All three of were having a great laugh within minutes of meeting. We worked our way through all the usual topics such as the weather, pub prices and that sort of thing before we got onto football.

This gave John his chance to plug our book about the senior football grounds we had visited a couple of years ago. He mentioned a couple of the bigger teams before straying onto the smaller fry like Peterhead. I have no idea why he chose to talk about that particular team but it seemed to strike a chord with Brian.

John demonstrates why old guys shouldn't take strong drink

He said that he had seen a few games up there. This surprised me as I happen to know that even the locals don't turn out all that often to see their team. That might have something to do with the Artic conditions which prevail up there. But when he mentioned some of the games being 30 a-side affairs that I started to pay attention. The penny finally dropped when he said that the referees were too feart to come on to the park even when a foul was committed.

Actually committed is the perfect word to use in this case. The football 'stadium' Brian was talking about was within the walls of Peterhead prison. And I was fairly sure that Brian had made the team on merit.

It seems that he had spent quite a long time enjoying free bed and board courtesy of Her Majesty. It could have been quite embarrassing, not to say dangerous, to ask a man what he had done to deserve a long stay in the slammer. But by this time we had had a number of pints of bravery and asked the question.

Fortunately Brian is a great guy and he didn't mind talking about his time behind bars.

In fact he told us it was all a bit of a misunderstanding. He had been sent down for 12 years for armed robbery. Although he admitted that he had indeed been carrying the sawn off shotgun he claimed that if he hadn't accidentally tripped over a piece of wood the gun would never have gone off. If it hadn't been for that trip the police would never have got the impression that he was shooting at them and the prison sentence might have been more lenient.

The jokes were flying by this time and I couldn't resist telling my one funny story about prison life. It goes something like this: Prisoners have it easy nowadays, three square meals a day and a good roof under their feet.

I rarely miss a chance to put my foot in things and today was a prime example of that talent. Brian had been involved in the Peterhead riots, which saw the prisoners take to the roof tops to demonstrate against conditions inside. I very nearly asked if they were complaining about lumpy porridge, but it seems that even I have limits. Brian was one of the chaps up on the roof rearranging the slates.

All of this was some time ago and Brian is on the straight and narrow nowadays. In fact there is a fair bit of irony at work here since he has found gainful employment with the council, as a slater.

It's a job he seems well qualified for as it is on record that he has a good head for heights. What pleases him most about the job is that although he does need to wear a hard hat, he no longer needs to wear a balaclava or gloves.

During a break in the conversation we were introduced to the Manager of *Raffles*, Karen Younger and the barmaid Anjela Nichols. They were a bit of a double act and filled us in on the goings on in the pub.

Anjela and Karen

We were telling them how much we liked their pub when Karen announced that *Raffles* was the biggest and best sports bar in Dunfermline. Before either John or I could point out that there was apparently only one television in the place Brian decided to weigh in, saying "Sports Bar! We canny even get BBC1 in here."

As sports bars go this one is definitely my favourite. It is certainly the friendliest one I've ever been in.

Although I was certain that *Raffles* was not going to turn out to be the oldest boozer in Dunfermline I had a hunch that it was a good age.

The shape and size of the front windows suggested to me that the building could well be early Victorian. So I was fairly confident of a good result when I asked the girls behind the bar if they could tell me when the pub first opened its doors.

I thought John was going to laugh himself sick when Karen said that she thought the pub first opened in 1976. To make matters worse Anjela said that before then it had actually been a Chinese restaurant.

After hearing that, I decided that the only thing to do was launch myself into a wee bit of a binge drinking session.

Despite making a bit of a fool of myself I thoroughly enjoyed our visit. With a name like *Raffles* I had been a wee bit worried that we would find ourselves wandering into a wine bar.

Nothing could be further from the truth. Raffles is an excellent example of a working man's pub. The beer is good and reasonably priced. It is comfortable and the patter was great.

If only it had been a couple of hundred years older things would have been perfect. But you can't have everything, I suppose.

As far as that other establishment we visited, for all of 30 seconds, is concerned I can definitely say it would benefit from an extra bit of signage. If there are any under employed graffiti artists in the Dunfermline area they could do the beer loving public a big favour. By simply adding a single word to the name above the door of that pub, a lot of confusion and trauma could be avoided.

Just in case you can't guess, the word is GO.

John's Comments; Craig is not even trying to claim this is an old pub, but it one that is worth a visit, and if Craig or I lived in Dunfermline, I am sure this would be our local. It is a nut house. We both loved it, the staff and the crazy locals. Especially our new friend Brian, who should be back inside serving time for attempting to murder us with his patter. A pub that is well worth a visit next time you are in Dunfermline. The drink is also the cheapest in town-but good quality, real Smirnoff and everything.

John; Homeward bound; Amazingly, we both felt reasonably sober when we left Dunfermline Bus Station, and a good sleep on the bus meant we arrived back in Glasgow feeling in good spirits, but with a bit of a thirst. This, and the fact that we had an hour to wait before we could get the cheap 90p ticket on the train, meant that we had little option other than to have two or three wee swallies in Glasgow before heading home to EK.

find oor Auld Boozers
by Bus . . . .

The X24, 26 or 27 will all take you to Dunfermline from Buchanan Street in just over an hour. Same buses back. You will get one of them every 20 minutes or so.

. . . . then by Boot
The Old Inn

Go out the back of the bus station and when you get onto High Street walk sown the hill to the right. Kirkgate is on the left and the pub is about 50 yards on the right.

Raffles Sports Bar

Go back onto the High Street, walk to the end of it and carry on to Bridge Street. Raffles is about 100 yards on the right.

Stirling

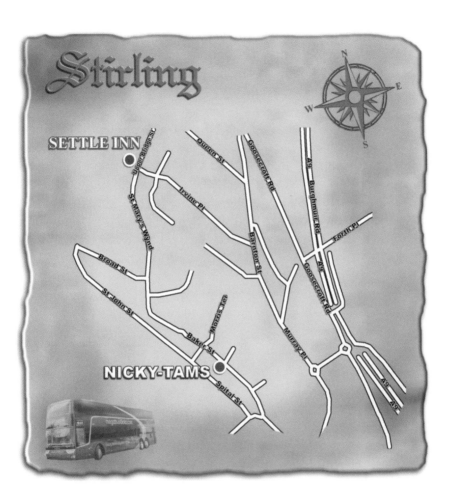

John; Land of Wallace, Bruce and Bannockburn, one of Scotland's most historical towns, and we felt sure there would be some old boozers with battle-hardened locals, or even some old locals in battle-hardened boozers!

Up in the area of the Castle, in the old town, I knew there were a few historic pubs. But which was the oldest? As usual,

Craig took the fun out of finding the oldest by using the computer, so he bagged the one it came up with.

It's a short 40 minute or so run up to Stirling on the M8 coach, which is on its way to Dundee. This straightforward run saw us arrive in Stirling Bus Station about noon. Craig took the lead and I followed him to our first, and he thought oldest pub in Stirling. But only time would tell.

Craig's 1st Pub; *The Settle Inn; The Settle Inn* in Stirling is without doubt one of the most atmospheric pubs I've ever visited. I should really qualify that statement. It was exactly what I have always had in my mind's eye when I think about quaint old Scottish pubs. It is totally authentic; there were no daft or dodgy bits added to the decor to artificially age the pub. Everything about the place gives the impression of an ancient but well-run bar.

John makes himself comfortable in the Settle Inn

We were the first customers of the day so we got to monopolise the time of the landlady, Leslie Beech. She told us that

The Settle Inn was indeed the oldest pub in Stirling and quite possibly the region.

Although the property has recently been renovated, wisely it has not been modernised out of recognition.

As soon as we got through the door I knew that it was my kind of pub: you can almost taste the history. The back lounge has a fairly unusual arched ceiling. Actually it reminded me of all those businesses which trade out of the shops built under the railway arches in Glasgow. But apparently the lounge was at one time a stable with the entrance at the rear of the building. As far as I was concerned this was proof if proof were needed that the Settle Inn was a really old pub.

Leslie will make sure you 'settle in'

The website I had visited had been quite clear about the lineage of the pub in fact they had rather cheekily referred to one of the pubs we had visited much earlier in our search for the oldest pubs in the country.

If you key in a request to find oldest pub in Scotland you will probably come across an entry citing the Clachan in Drymen. It claims not only to be the oldest pub in Scotland but reveals to the watchers of the world-wide-web that it dates from 1734. The previous owner of the Settle Inn writing on the pub's web site asks "Is 1733 not older than 1734?"

Even John could be expected to work that one out, depending on what time of the day you ask him of course.

I did notice that the fonts for the pub's own-brand beers had 1733 emblazoned across them, just in case there was any question in your mind about the pub's history.

We asked our usual questions about odd and, or humorous activity in the pub, expecting the usual stories about hijinks at the Hallowe'en party et cetera, but Leslie told us about one of those incident which only seem to happen in the type of pub John and I prefer to frequent.

It seems two old boys had a bit of a set-to one night. That's not particularly unusual you might say, but the gentlemen in question were both at the dangerous end of their 70s. Not only that but both were partially disabled requiring walking sticks.

That last fact proved to be a bit unfortunate for one of them as in the front car he was knocked unconscious by his opponent's walking aid. John said there must be something in the water up in Stirling but I'm pretty sure that it was the lack of water in their drinks that led to the trouble.

I did ask Leslie if it was okay to use the old boys' names since we didn't want to embarrass them when the book came out. But she assured me that it would be fine since one of the old yins is barred for life and the other one is dead, so no chance of a libel case then! I don't really seem to know what the fight was about but I like to think there was a woman involved.

Inevitably the subject of ghosts came up. I have my suspicions about who steered the conversation in that direction and one of these days I will get him back for it.

Leslie told us that she had witnessed an odd occurrence in the pub a few years back.

The story as I remembered it concerned a customer who apparently lost his way on the road to or from the gent's toilet. It seems that he found himself in the cellar where he saw a ghostly figure washing the dishes in the sink. He was so shocked that he ran from the pub vowing never to return. Just to put the ghostly icing on the cake, Leslie told us there was in fact no sink in the cellar.

John was suitably impressed with the story, deploying his 'You don't say' face.

I was not impressed on so many levels. I can of course understand his shock at seeing the woman washing the dishes in the sink. It must be about 20 years since I personally witnessed Irene doing the dishes in the sink and that's not just because we've got a dishwasher. Secondly I wandered around the pub and it took about three minutes. It's tiny. Anyone who can manage to get lost in such a small place cannot be trusted as a witness to do anything. Even John after a serious bevy session couldn't manage to misplace the ground floor. It is obvious the bloke in question had been indulging in some heavyweight boozing or even a bit of recreational smoking.

It is equally obvious that his vow never to return should be seen as a good thing. Some other poor buggers will now have to put up with his craziness. Besides which, just how menacing is it an act of witnessing dishes being washed? I could see the force of it if this visitor from beyond was chucking the dishes at him but that was never mentioned.

It never ceases to amaze me how many nutters there are on the loose. Leslie told us that the Settle had been visited by a group of ghost hunters. Calling themselves 'The Ghost Circle', the leader of this band of heroes obviously had a touch of the dramatics about him as he swanned around the pub in a large hat and carrying a walking stick which for reasons known only to him had a large feather attached to it. He also favoured a long flowing cloak it seems. I'm not sure why he thought he needed to dress up like this, but I'm fairly sure he didn't do it to blend in with the rest of the clientele in the pub.

I asked what this Sherlock Holmes of the ghostie world found, although I was pretty sure that I already knew what the answer would be.

They didn't find any actual ghosts, I wasn't shocked to hear, but they did find definite indications of 'a presence'. If you believe in this guff then there probably is a presence, and that will be the presence of a zip in the back of your heid!

If they really want to spend their time trying to understand life's great mysteries they should do what the rest of us do and drink more than is good for you while watching channel 4 late at night.

Billy and his twa dugs settle doon in The Settle Inn

In conclusion, The Settle Inn is definitely the oldest boozer in Stirling without a doubt. Any nonsense to the contrary that John comes up with will be laughable. I was very impressed with the layout of the pub, which has the look and feeling of a country pub. I suppose at one time it probably was one.

There is not a hint of veneer in the entire place. As far as I could tell remains true to its original state. Take note Wetherspoons!

It is well within walking distance of the bus station; just take your time going up that hill. If it is not already on the Stirling tourist trail, it should be.

John's comments; It's an old pub right enough; 1733 is a hell of a long time ago and the landlady Leslie told us it was a Coaching Inn and cheese-making cheddary before that (is cheddary a real word?). I'll have to go some to beat it. Must admit it was a brilliant pub. My only hope of beating it came from Billy the two-dog owner who told me on the QT that there was a pub over the hill and down the hill (it's a hilly place). The pub is called Nicky Tam's *and he assured me it's a fairly ancient place, so that's where I was taking Craig next.*

John's 1st Pub; *Nicky Tam's;* A bit breathless, but with me full of hope, we found *NT's* no bother. As soon as we went in, I had hope in my heart that this could be a really old place, because it looked really old.

Nicky Tams, Stirling

The girls behind the bar, Lexy Reid and Nicole Pinkerton, were great company and told us all about the pub and that it in fact was a really old pub. I couldn't place Lexy's accent, and when I asked her she told me that she was from America and moved to Stirling when she married a Scots guy. Still had the accent, which was lovely. But back to the story. The girls couldn't put an exact date on the pub, but knew that it was at least 200 years old. Now this is old, but as Craig was happy to point out, it was not as old as his pub. This did not put me off as I could feel in my water that there was something about this pub that would make it of more historic interest than *The Settle Inn,* if not actually older, which, at the end of the day is not that important, unless you are Craig.

Nicole and Lexy, Tams international barmaids

I asked the girls what the name of the pub meant. Nicole told me that Nicky Tams were special knickers that were worn in the old days, especially in Aberdeen, to stop beasties running up your leg and invading your private parts. I never found out why Aberdeen was the area where this was a common garment. If you believe the stories you hear from comedians nowadays, it's the sheep that should be wearing them. Only kidding Aberdonians. I asked why a pub in Stirling should have such a name, the girls told me that the reason they thought the pub got this name was that long ago, many of its customers were real beasties, a bit like today.

The most exciting information we learned came from Nicole, who told us that it was her Great Great Grandfather who

210

founded the Pinkerton Detective Agency in America. This alone makes it the oldest pub in Stirling where a descendant opened the oldest detective agency in the world. Surely this should put it in the running for the oldest pub.

Other tremendous information we got from the girls was that the pub had been called *The Caledonian Vaults* and before that *Dukes Bar,* not only that but that it has been voted the third best pub in Scotland in the STV Entertainment Awards programme. Craig's pub was nowhere. Also, in 1999, it was voted the most haunted bar in Stirling. Craig's pub didn't have a ghost of a chance against *Nicky Tams*.

I asked Nicole and Lexy if they had ever encountered a ghost, as a first-hand account is always more believable. One night, Nicole told me, she was downstairs checking on the toilets before closing up and one of the doors was locked. She waited a few minutes and eventually shouted for the woman, who she assumed was drunk and asleep, because she could hear loud snoring. Nothing happened. She was about to go for help when the door opened and when she looked inside, the toilet was empty. Nicole told me she had to use the toilet herself right away!

Nicole and Ben

One of the locals in the bar, Ben Goodall, told me about the picture that was hanging on the wall. It's of an old minister called Ian Campbell, and the photograph was found in the cellar many years ago. Assuming it was an important figure from the pubs past, it was hung in the bar. Since that day, strange things, even a murder, have happened in the bar. 'Why don't you take it down' I asked. 'We're all terrified of the way he looks at you', said Nicole. It's true stories like that that make our journeys worthwhile.

Nicky Tam's is a great bar and well worth a visit if you are ever in Stirling. I've got to admit that Craig's bar may be the actual oldest in years, and a great bar as well, but old *NT's* is the oldest in many other ways, if you know what I mean.

Craig's comments; *I actually voted against visiting this pub, but as usual John didn't bother listening to me.*

And for once he did the right thing. My only objection to going in there was the fact that we had visited this pub for an earlier book.

Luckily the place had changed since that time, and it now looked like a completely different place. A bit too modern for my taste but the friendly bar-staff more than made up for that little annoyance.

I remembered that on our last time in this bar I had taken the time to explain to John the meaning of the pubs name.

Nicky Tams were the strings farm labourers tied around their trouser legs, just below the knee, to stop rats attaching themselves to the more delicate areas found above the knee.

You would expect a horror story like that would stay with a man; but not John. It seems I was wasting my time. While standing up at the bar trying to impress the young barmaids I heard him explain to them that Nicky Tams were in fact special trousers made for farmers.

I toyed with the idea of setting him right but decided that it would be more fun taking the piss after he wrote about it. Mission accomplished!

John; **Homeward journey;** We had a brilliant time and great hospitality in both bars, meaning we left Stirling very happy. The bus journey home, as usual, passed in a flash.

Find oor Auld Boozers

by Bus . . . .

The M8 Bus from Buchanan Street Bus Station, non-stop, right into Stirling Bus Station.

. . . . then by Boot

The Settle Inn

You leave the bus station and walk up Burnton Street away from the town centre, with the train line on your right. I think it's second on the left up Irvine Place, which is a hell of a steep hill. The pub is at the end of the street, on St. Mary's Wynd.

Nicky Tam's

Turn right when you leave *The Settle Inn*, carry on up and over St. Mary's Wynd, you go onto Bow Street and then Baker Street, *Nicky Tam's* is on the right. It's not as long a walk as it sounds'

Ayr

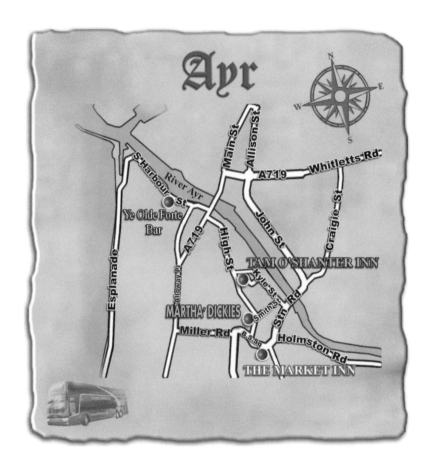

John: A toon that Burn's made famous for its honest men and bonny lassies, but are there any old pubs, and if there are, which is the oldest, and will anyone be honest about it, and did Burn's ever drink in it? We hope to answer all these questions and many more in this chapter.

But first we had to have a starting point. As ever, Craig used his assortment of high tec. phones, laptops and other gadgetry to come up with what the internet told him was Ayr's oldest pub. The answer was *The Black Bull*. It was just the day before our trip that he discovered the pub had been closed due to a fire destroying part of the roof and other things. It may be the oldest pub, but it's shut!

This minor problem didn't stop Craig. The web came up with *Tam O' Shanter Inn* as the new oldest pub in Ayr, so he said he would take that one as his first pub. The man has no shame. As usual, I said that I'd make it up as we went along. So on a glorious sunny morning in March, we hared down to Ayr, delivered some books to Waterstone's, crossed the High Street, and found the pub in no time at all. In we went to the Inn.

Tam O Shanter Inn, Ayr

Craig 1ˢᵗ pub: When it was decided that we would be exploring the town of Ayr I immediately laid claim to *The Black Bull Inn* as my first choice of pub to write about. Being from the area I knew *The Black Bull* is generally accepted as being the oldest hostelry in town.

John, being from one of the grimmer areas of Glasgow, had no idea about Ayr's vintage drinking dens.

To add to my already vast knowledge on this subject I decided to do a little extra research, just in case I had somehow overlooked some small detail. As usual I had waited to the last possible moment before doing so.

Customer John Furey and Anne our friendly barmaid

The night before our trip I sat down at my computer and was almost immediately confronted by a rather large snag. Right there on the screen was a recent newspaper article about the pub I had chosen to visit. Even without reading the article it was clear that I would have to change my plans. The accompanying picture showed several fire engines parked outside the pub and I couldn't help but notice that there didn't seem to be a roof on the building.

On the bus down to Ayr the next morning I mentioned to John that I had changed my mind and would rather take *The Tam O' Shanter Inn* as my first pub of the day. Since he seemed quite pleased with the switch I didn't bother mentioning the unfortunate and badly timed fire incident until we actually got off the bus.

The pub which became *The Tam O' Shanter Inn* dates from long ago. It eventually got its name from the famous poem by Robert Burns, but it started out as a brewery. Apart from a short stint as a museum, it has been slaking the thirst of many a generation of drouthy Ayr tipplers ever since.

I can actually remember when it was a museum. From the outside it looked a bit too dry and dusty for the likes of me so I never crossed its threshold. So our visit today would be the first time I've ever been in the place, I think I was probably expecting to find it a bit of an up market Rabbie Burns thing pub. Happily that was not the case. Although there is very definitely a theme to the place it is never overstated.

It is a real working pub with real drinkers enjoying a Friday afternoon tipple. There is a huge open fireplace at the end of the bar just as you enter. Even though it was an unseasonably warm afternoon we just had to have a seat next to the hearth. It was very atmospheric. After a few minutes, though it was time to get back to work, there were pints to be drunk and people to be chatted to.

The barmaid, Anne Scott, was very helpful and searched the pub to find a book about the history of the *Tam O' Shanter Inn*. She also scoured the bar to find someone to help us with stories about the place.

However, as soon as they found out that I was from nearby Auchinleck the customers preferred to spend their time slagging me off. To be fair they also slagged off every other town in Ayrshire, so I didn't get too paranoid about it.

Tam's is a world famous pub, mostly because of the association with Burns and his poem about Tam O' Shanter. Legend has it that Rabbie based his work on real characters he encountered while taking the odd pint of wine in his local.

There are several versions of what was really behind the story of Tam and if you spend enough time and money in the pub you will probably hear all of them. My particular favourite one is that the whole story of witches and galloping horses was just an elaborate cover story for the hero's overindulgence in the pub one dark night. People must have been a hell of a lot more gullible back then if they thought this excuse would ever get a drunk off the hook with his wife.

Davie Cowan came over to talk to us and we asked him if he could recommend another old pub in Ayr for us to visit. Without a moment's hesitation, he suggested that we should make our way round to the Market Inn. He told us that it was a fine old pub which had survived all the best efforts of the developers to knock it down and replace it with something modern and soulless.

Davie did seem to know quite a bit about the Market, from history to current bar staff and even individual local worthies. As it turns out, he actually owns *The Market* as well as *Tam O' Shanters*. This could have been seen as a conflict of interest to us but since he bought us a round of drinks we decided to take his advice and include *The Market* in our summary of fine old Scottish pubs.

We were thinking about making a move as we had a full day ahead of us. Although it is quite possible that John just wanted to go before he had to buy a round. Before we could take leave of the place one of the pub's off duty barmen came over to speak to us.

Anthony McBride had just nipped in to check when he was supposed to be working, and had been sent over to talk to us by Anne. We had a few laughs about some of the customers he has had to deal with over the years. My favourite story concerned one of his better off customers.

This chap had wandered into the pub about lunchtime on Christmas Eve. He had been out shopping for something for the big dinner next day. Apparently it was his family tradition to have venison on the table at Christmas. His only task that day was to pick up the large cut of venison from the butchers and take it home. Unfortunately the festive spirit got a hold of him and he decided to have a couple of drinks with his pals in Tam's. Not wanting to leave the costly meat sitting in the bar he asked Anthony if he could put it in the fridge while he enjoyed his drink. That of course was a big mistake as the barman decided to play a trick on the guy and instead of handing him back his plastic bag containing the venison he switched it to a sleeve of Lorne sausage.

Everyone expected the bloke to come roaring back into the pub a few minutes after leaving to give them a piece of his mind for switching the meat.

It was a few hours before they were contacted by the man's wife. Apparently the bloke had continued drinking when he got home and it wasn't until his wife checked the bag that the sausage was found. Instead of seeing it as a pub joke, in a series of drunken phone calls, he accused the butcher of making a mistake and threatened to sue him as he had destroyed their Christmas.

Apparently there was very little goodwill in his household that year.

John's comments; No complaints from me on Craig's Shanter. It's a lovely wee pub and the staff and locals were great company. But, as usual, I was making a nuisance of myself with the locals and asking questions about the history of the pub. An interesting fact I learned is that the Shanter was opened as a pub about 250 years ago, fair enough. But for a period of time in the 50s it was a Museum. It then re-opened as a pub. Does it still have a claim as Ayr's oldest pub. Make up your own minds. It's a great wee pub no matter how old it is. Before we left I had to find a pub to go to next. I asked Davie Cowan, the owner of the Shanter if he knew another old pub. Not only did he say he knew one of the oldest pub's in Ayr, he owned it as well. Was he telling the truth, or did he just want us to spend money in his other pub? Having said that, he had just bought us a round, so the guy must have been telling the truth. Thus we headed to Davie's other pub next, The Market Inn.

The Market Inn, Ayr

220

John's 1ˢᵗ pub; *The Market Inn;* It was only a five minute walk up High Street, across a couple of streets, and we found the pub standing proudly on its own. The land around it had been re-developed by Morrison's, but The Market is a listed building, so the developers couldn't touch it, and glad we were they didn't. It's a brilliant pub.

The inside is just as interesting as the outside. It has a fantastic island bar and dozens of original features that gives the place a great atmosphere.

The barmaid, Rhea Scobie, made us feel really welcome, as did the locals, who filled us in with tales of the pub. The photograph Craig has taken will show you what a fine looking group they are.

Billy,Rhea, Murray, Jimmy and bringing up the rear, Jim (sun Glasses)

One of the older regulars, Owen Kerr, told me all about the history of the pub, and how it was the Cattle Market Bar in the old days of Cattle Markets. Cows and sheep were regular sights in and around the pub.

On a sadder note, the locals showed us a plaque above the bar in memory of Lord Charles Kennedy, who was chief of the Clan Kennedy. Unfortunately, he recently had a heart attack and died during a trip to the States. He was a regular and the plaque is positioned above the bar stool he sat in. I knew he wouldn't mind if I had a wee shot in it. I am a member of the Mackay Clan after all.

The drinks, and time, were passing quickly, and Craig wanted to head down to the harbour area where he knew there were a couple of pubs that may qualify as the oldest. So we said our goodbyes to the locals, and following instructions, we went round the corner and got the number three bus down to the harbour area. It would have been quicker walking, but Craig was knackered.

Craig's comments: The Market Inn *is a great pub. I can't actually find anything to complain about, and as you know I'm a bit of an expert when it comes to nit-picking and fault finding. The best laugh of the day came when one of the guys in the pub gave us the explanation of exactly how he had come about his facial injuries: "St. Patrick's Day and gravity!"*

Ye Olde Forte Bar, Ayr

Craig's 2nd Pub: One of the lads in *The Market Inn* suggested that we try *Ye Olde Forte Bar*, down by the harbour. To be honest I thought he was taking the mickey, but since it wasn't too far away from the bus station we decided to give it a go.

Despite its name *Ye Olde Forte* is a very modern looking pub, very bright and airy. We were served by the owner, Carol Ward, who told us about her pub.

222

Historically speaking the Old Forte is situated within the walls of what was once a Citadel built by Oliver Cromwell back in the old days. Some sections of the original walls can still be seen further down the street from the pub. If that is not cool enough for you there is evidence that the greatest of Scotland's Patriots, William Wallace, is connected with this particular area of the town. He certainly stopped off long enough to murder the English garrison which was stationed there. And before you say he was just doing a bit of freedom fighting you should remember that the troops he killed had surrendered before he decided to burn them to death.

In more recent times, because of its position in South Harbour Street the pub benefited from all the trade from fishing boats and the nearby fish market.

Carol has only been in charge of the pub since July 2014 but is making great efforts to build up a customer base. She told us that when she started out she had one beer font, one keg of beer and very little of anything else. To make a go of it will take a lot of determination. Fortunately Carol has plenty of that.

This kind of thing just suits John to a T

Before she took over in *Ye Olde Forte,* the pub had been getting a bad reputation. In fact the licence had been suspended after reports of after-hours drinking and general rowdyism.

One of the customers told me that he had been drinking in the pub back then and often didn't need to spend an awful lot of money to enjoy a good night out. It seems that the former manager had a tendency towards generosity, especially later in the evening. On one occasion the customer had been served seven pints but only charged for one. Even John could see that this was not a great business plan. Apparently the former manager is no longer active in the licenced trade. If just half the stories we heard about him are true then he has probably ceased being active entirely.

Thankfully since taking over the pub, Carol, and her partner Alastair Goodwin, have turned things around and now Ye Olde Forte Bar is a popular and profitable venue.

We enjoyed a couple of drinks and chatted with Carol and some of her customers before it was time to hurry back to the bus station.

John's comments: *Craig's second pub, situated down at the harbour is a very friendly one. The owner Carol is great fun and it is a pub well worth a visit if you're ever down that way. No complaints from me.*

Matha' Dickies, Ayr

John's 2nd pub: *Matha Dickies Pub;* While we were walking up towards *The Market Bar*, we went round a bend and there was a wee pub stuck away in a corner. Craig, who knows Ayr and its pubs very well, had never seen or heard of this pub. It was a really unusual looking place from the outside. I decided spontaneously to live on the edge and take this as my second pub of the day. Could it be the oldest? I didn't care, so in we went.

Fiona Morrison

The barmaid, Fionna Morrison, was outside having a fag as we eyed the place up, and followed us in. Fionna told us that this pub had been on this site for only 10 years. Before that it was called *Peppers*. I couldn't find out what the total time was that the two pubs had been in existence. To be honest, I wasn't that bothered. It is a nice wee pub, if you can find it. Its only claim to fame that I could find out is that a band called 'The Mauraders' sometimes play there. It's a quirky wee place and we enjoyed our pint before moving on to the real old pubs.

Craig's comments; We very nearly missed this pub. The door is at the far end of a small cul-de-sac. Going in was just pure nosiness on our part as neither of us were really sure that there was a pub beyond that door.

While it is definitely nowhere near being the oldest pub in toon, Matha Dickies is a good old fashioned, no frills boozer.

Find oor Auld Boozers

by Bus . . . .

It's an easy run from Glasgow. The X76 from Buchanan Street Bus Station runs regularly, and will get you there in under an hour.

. . . . then by Boot

Tam O' Shanters Inn
Get off the bus from Glasgow the stop after it goes over the river, it's the stop before the bus station, and walk up the High Street, it's on your left. You can't miss it.

The Market Inn
Turn left up High Street and follow the road round till you get to Castlehill Road. You will see the big Morrison's store behind it.

Ye Old Fort Bar
Go back down to the river and walk down the left bank (a bit like Paris) and you will find it no bother. The street is called South Harbour Street.

Martha Dickie's Bar
This is a funny wee pub stuck away up a wee alley. If you go up to the top of High Street and then round a sort of bend going right, it will appear on your right.

Broughty Ferry for Dundee

John; Today we were heading to Dundee to find its oldest pub, or get pissed trying.

Using his high tech, web-based gizmos, Craig came to the conclusion that the oldest pubs in Dundee were in Broughty Ferry. I was a bit concerned with this information, but Craig assured me that he had checked, and Brought Ferry has been part of Dundee since 1913. I don't know if the locals were too happy about it.

Accuracy and details have never been a great interest of mine, so I was happy to be heading to the Broughty area of Dundee.

We had been to Dundee many times so the journey was straight-forward enough. The only laugh I gave Craig was when we got on the bus from outside Dundee Bus Station to take us to Broughty Ferry. I put down my bus pass and told the driver where we were heading. I heard him reply 'Conductron'. I thought this was where the bus was going and was in the middle of asking him where it was when Craig banged me on the shoulder and explained that the driver had said 'Conductor on'. Craig, coming from deepest Ayrshire, is better at weird dialects than me.

After Craig stopped laughing, we had an enjoyable wee run to Broughty Ferry. It's a lovely place which looks as if there are a lot of really well-off people living in it.

We got off our No. 73 in the centre of the town, wandered down to the front and found the pub that Craig had picked as he thought it was the oldest.

Craig's 1st Pub; *The Ship;* We have visited Dundee quite a few times over the last few years, and have enjoyed the odd beer along the way. On this our latest trip up there we decided to check out a particular area that so far we had never considered: Broughty Ferry.

As a destination Broughty Ferry was a bit of a blank canvas to us piss-artists, but we were more than willing to go there and paint the town red.

The journey up was incident free, if you don't count John making an arse of himself on the bus from Dundee city centre to 'Broughty'.

Our first pub of the day was *The Ship Inn* on Fisher Street. I had decided to look for the oldest pub down by the edge of the River Tay. It seemed logical to me that the first houses in the area would probably be built down there. After all, the river provided a convenient transport route and a ready source of food in the fish to be taken from it. And as we all know, when a fishing community springs up, sooner rather than later, one of the cottages will be converted into a pub. Fishermen tend to like a drink or two after a hard day's netting. There was once a regular boat service from Dundee over to this community. I imagine that's what put the ferry in Broughty.

The Ship Inn, Broughty Ferry

The Ship Inn has been in business for a couple of hundred years, so we are told. It certainly looks the part, as the pub itself is within a small two storey detached building. The bar is on the ground floor while the restaurant upstairs offers a perfect view of the River Tay through a single panoramic window.

We were very impressed with the traditional décor in the pub. The bar has an unusual shape, with large carved figures, reminiscent of ships' figureheads, incorporated into it.

Our barmaid, Amanda Speedie introduced us to *The Ship's* owner, Steve Cummings, who has been in charge for about 10 years. Steve told us that it had always been his ambition to own The Ship. As a young man out on the town with his friends he used to enjoy the occasional pint in this pub. But unlike them had a plan to one day own the place and not just drink it dry.

Finding the exact age of the pub proved a bit too much for us but Steve was pretty sure that *The Ship* was one of the oldest pubs in Broughty Ferry. As evidence he told us about what was found when the pub was last renovated. It seems that when the floor boards were lifted the workers discovered that the building had very little in the way of foundations. Just below the floor they found a layer of pebbles. The house had quite literally been built on the shore of the river. Apparently the weight of the building helps to keeps it stable.

Steve, 'The Ship's' captain

We were shown a photo, taken in the late 19th century, of the area around Fisher Street. The front row of houses, seen in the picture, was demolished to allow a wider road to be built along the shore of the river.

Not only did this help traffic flow but it also provided *The Ship* with the unobstructed view of The Tay which so many of the restaurant's customers appreciate today.

While talking to Steve, we discovered that he has owned and renovated a few other pubs in the area. Fortunately, for those of us who appreciate good old fashioned boozers, once he acquired *The Ship Inn* he realised that it needed to be kept as it was, totally untouched by mood lighting or fake Mackintosh furniture.

I'm pretty sure that John does it just to annoy me now, but he asked Steve and Amanda if there was a pub ghost. This sort of nonsense shouldn't be encouraged, but fortunately the good folks of Broughty Ferry are far too sensible to fall for any of that kind of keech. John's daft question was dismissed.

While we were having a laugh at the bar we were introduced to one of the pub's regulars, George Allan. He lives locally and is a bit of an expert on Junior football. Given that we recently brought out our book on Junior football we had plenty to talk about.

Amanda and regular customer George

Added to that, my local team, Auchinleck Talbot, had just won the Scottish Junior Cup and I felt the need to talk to someone who actually knew about the game. John tries his best but being a former Partick Thistle supporter he has lost all notion of how to deal with cup final success, or even winning three games on the trot.

Usually we try to limit ourselves to a couple of beers per pub when we are out and about on a fact-finding mission. Of course there are exceptions to this rule, and a combination of good beer, great surroundings and the opportunity to get in a bit of bragging about my football team meant that this was one of those exceptions.

An indication of how well the booze was flowing came when Steve offered to buy us something to eat from his pub's extensive menu. He was getting a bit concerned that we might not manage to see out the day in anything like a fit state if we didn't take some food on board.

This proved two things to me: 1) He had no faith in the drinking abilities of your average West Coast man, and 2), Much more seriously, it was obvious that he had never read any of our books.

We declined his kind offer and asked the assembled company if they could recommend any other pubs in the town which might be as old as, if not older than *The Ship*.

Two suggestions were put forward: *The Fisherman's Tavern* and *The Eagle*. We gratefully accepted the challenge and said our farewells.

John's comments; *It is a beautiful pub right on the front with great views across the river Tay. The owner, and the locals were all very nice and we had a brilliant time. But is it the oldest? An old worthy I was talking to told me that there were a couple of others that could be older. This is what I liked, getting one over on Craig in the oldest pub stakes. I mentioned them to Craig and he agreed we would visit both.*

John's 1st Pub; *Fisherman's Tavern and Hotel;* As soon as we walked in we knew this was a brilliant pub. Everything in it was to our taste, a low ceiling, no kids or families and a brilliant bar. Altogether a very atmospheric haven for the older traveller

Tracy Cooper, the manager, was brilliant company, and when we told her of our quest, filled us in with the history and story of this great wee pub. The first thing she told us was the pub opened in 1827, which made it 20 years older than Craig's *Ship*.

Craig's depression was lifted when the honest Tracey told us that although *The Fisherman's* was quite old, there was another pub in the town that may be even older. Before she even got the name of the pub out, Craig claimed it for his next pub. More about it later.

Another interesting thing about *The Fisherman'*s is that it is the only pub in Scotland to feature in Camra's Real Ale Pubs list from 1975-2009, without a break. The pub also has an original 'Snug'-and a lounge bar at the back. It's the sort of pub where you are always finding wee corners for another drink. There are also 12 rooms to let. It would a brilliant place for a long weekend.

Tracy, the manager of The Fisherman's Tavern

We usually end up talking to any locals who are holding up the bar, and this pub was no exception. John Cunningham, a vest wearing local worthy filled us in with amazing facts about the area, and the pub. Among the ones I remember (and it's amazing I can remember anything) is that the Lifeboat at the bottom of the street is one of the busiest in the UK. Apart from the normal things you would expect from a river like the Tay, which has the biggest volume of water flowing down it of any river in Britain, there are, unfortunately, a few jumpers from the Tay Bridges just up the river a bit.

A couple of amazing historical facts we learned from John is that Dundee is the second oldest place in Britain, after York, in terms of Medieval Cities. Another is that, and I bet nobody knows

233

this, because of Dundee's link with the Jute trade and the country of India, if you have a day off work, it's called 'A Bombay Fast'. Now admit it, you didn't know that. Unfortunately, now you do.

I love unusual historical facts like these, and John ended up giving me a book about the History of Dundee. What a man! Not only that, we got round to talking about what he did to kill his day, and did he not disappear for a few minutes and return with a huge bucket full of whelks and crabs. John explained that these were Pillar Crabs, which are the best bait in the world. I suddenly realised that he enjoyed a bit of fishing in his spare time. He even demonstrated the Crabs ability to get out of its Shell. To be honest, I could have happily missed that bit.

Just good friends John and John

When I mentioned to John that my Kate (the wife and luckiest woman in the world) loved whelks, he disappeared again, only to return with a bag of them, all cleaned, salted and cooked. Kate loved them, ate them all at the one sitting the next morning. Kate sends her thanks John.

Another lovely pair of semi-locals we met were Lorraine and Alex Christie, who love nothing more than a walk from Dundee out to this great wee pub.

We could have stayed there all day, but Craig was keen to visit our next, and last pub, which Tracy had told us might be even older. I know one thing; it may be older, but it won't be a better bar. That would be impossible!

So we said our goodbyes, and thanks, to Tracy (who also bought three of our books) as well as John and the rest of the locals, and headed out to find our last, and Craig's second pub.

Craig's comments; What a great pub. Actually it was more like three pubs. I don't know about it being the oldest in town, but it was a fantastic place-great staff and beer, definitely my kind of pub.

Craig's 2ⁿᵈ Pub; *The Eagle Coaching Inn;* Even without seeing it I knew that I wanted The Eagle to be one of the pubs I got to write about. For purely nostalgic reasons I felt that I should be the one who put pen to paper on this pub.

The reasoning behind my thinking is easily explained. My first drinking pub was called the Eagle Inn. It was in *The Eagle* that, as a boy, I learned how to hold my drink. Obviously there were some hiccups along the way, but I remember it fondly.

Given that my *Eagle* was in Auchinleck and it was the early 1970s you can imagine that it was a bit on the rough side. Unlike my early boozer, *The Eagle* in Broughty Ferry is a bright, airy and friendly place.

After ordering our first drink we got chatting to the barmaid, Abbie Lawson. She told us that *The Eagle* was a family-run hotel. The lease for the pub is owned by Debbie Findlay.

After a bit of the usual banter, which consists of us trying to convince the bar staff that we really are writing a book, and not just trying to cadge a free drink, we got onto the subject of pub history.

According to Debbbie, during renovations in the 1950s a horde of coins was found. The coins were dated up to 1636 and that suggests that there was some sort of business taking place within that building from that time.

If it was an inn then that would certainly make The Eagle or whatever it was called at the time the oldest pub in town. It certainly became a coaching inn during the mid1800s when a coach service was introduced to take locals to and from Dundee.

There had been a ferry service doing just that for many years previously but a rather shrewd businessman saw an opportunity to make a few bob. The ferry journey could be affected by the weather whereas the coach was a much safer bet.

During our conversation somebody asked if The Eagle had ever played host to any of the rich and famous. I think it was Abbie who mentioned that George Clooney had once visited the pub while on a golfing holiday.

Abbie and Debbie outside The Eagle

John chimed in at this point with a rather unlikely story. He claimed that he had once been mistaken for George Clooney. As you can imagine this revelation was met by a prolonged and awkward silence. Not many people get John's sense of humour. In fact that's pretty much 99.9 per cent of the population. To lighten the mood I suggested that he had misheard what was said and in fact he had been mistaken for George's aunt: Rosemary.

The only let down for me in *The Eagle* was the décor. It has recently been refurbished and now looks very modern indeed. As you know I prefer a more traditional set up, but I suppose it would be a bit odd if every pub in the town chose to stick with the old clapped-out look of the traditional Scottish boozer.

Please don't rush to point out that I only like this style because I am old and clapped-out myself. I only need to glance over at John to be reminded of that fact.

It is a bit strange, though, that the oldest pub in town now looks like the newest one, internally at least.

That being said, they certainly know how to have good old-fashioned fun in this pub. Some of the antics they have gotten up to have achieved international recognition via You-Tube.

On one of their latest escapades some of the regulars thought it would be a bit of a hoot to tie the barmaid to a chair and then lock her in the cellar.

Strangely, Debbie, the barmaid in question also thought this was hilarious. Even after they forgot about her and left her in the cellar for a couple of hours.

I really like it when people tell us their humorous stories, but sometimes it would be preferable if they left some of them unsaid, for example, as a punchline to her cellar story Debbie told us that she had been left in the cellar for so long that she had ended up wetting herself.

As funny stories go I thought this one was a bit of a damp squib, but everyone in the bar howled with laughter. Apparently, like John, I have no sense of humour.

We had a couple more beers in *The Eagle* while I enjoyed listening to John grudgingly admit that once again I had chosen the Auldest Boozer in Toon.

John's comments; Craig may have discovered the actual oldest pub in Dundee, and the pub was good enough, but not a patch on my Fisherman's Tavern.

John; way home; We had a great day out in the Broughty Ferry part of Dundee, and I don't think I would be surprising any locals if I said it would be hard to find a nicer part of Dundee, or any other city or town in Scotland. The three pubs were all different, but all worth a visit, especially *The Ship* and *The Fisherman's*. No offence to *The Eagle,* which is the actual oldest, we think. If you disagree, write to us.

Our run home went by in a flash, as usual, we both slept all the way. It's a hard job, but someone's got to do it.

Find oor Auld Boozers

by Bus . . . .

From Glasgow's Buchanan Street Bus Station the M9 coach heading for Aberdeen got us to Dundee Bus Station in about an hour and a half. You go out the back of the Bus Station and a No. 73, or a couple of other numbers, will get you to Broughty Ferry in about 10 minutes or so.

. . . . then by Boot

The Ship
Get off the bus in Queen Street, and it's only a two or three minute walk down Fort Street to the front, turn left at the Lifeboat station and it's there on your right.

The Fisherman's Tavern Hotel
About 50 yards back up Fort Street. You can see the back entrance from *The Ship*

The Eagle Coaching Inn
Turn right out of *The Fishermans* and it's another 50 or so yards back up Fort Street.

238

Lossiemouth for Elgin

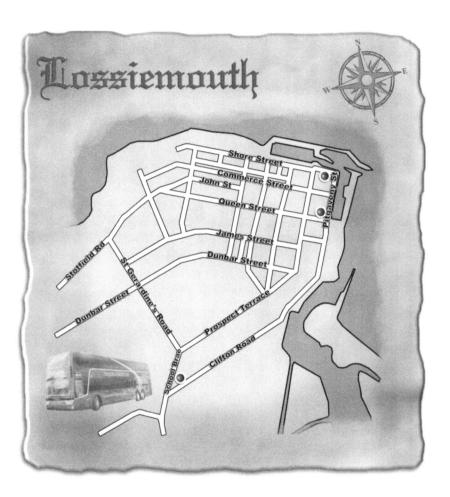

John; Picking Elgin as one of the places to find the oldest pub might surprise some of our readers, but not the more experienced ones who know that there's a Waterstone's in the town.

'Surely you're not just visiting towns in the hope of selling more books', I hear you say. 'You're damn right', I reply.

Craig is dead against visiting towns purely for financial reasons. 'Money buys drink', is my reply. This shuts him up.

When Craig looked for the oldest pubs in the Elgin area, he discovered they were in a wee town called Lossiemouth. I thought he was saying this so we would not go to Elgin again, but he assured me that he was telling the truth. He also said that as Lossiemouth was very near Elgin, we could claim it was in the Elgin Area. I caved in and said we would do as he wanted.

This led to another problem. Lossiemouth meant another bus journey which would mean we would have to leave Glasgow very early in the morning. The sacrificies we make for our work.

When I checked the Traveline web page, it told me that there was a 7.30am Gold Bus service to Inverness. There was also a 7.00 pm return Gold bus service from Inverness. It would be a hell of a long day as we would need to get a bus from Inverness to Elgin and then a local bus from Elgin to Lossiemouth. Normally my brother Robert who lives in Inverness would run us to and from Elgin, but he couldn't help today, so we were on our own, relying on local buses.

To cut to the chase, I booked us seats on the Gold Buses, found out the times of the local buses, and off we went. The wife (Kate) was kind enough to run us into Glasgow for the 7.30am Gold Bus. This meant getting up at six in the morning instead of god knows when if we would have had to catch the No. 18.

Because of the Gold Bus running a bit late, we arrived in Inverness Bus Station at 11.24 am, one minute before our No. 10 Aberdeen service was due to leave and drop us off in Elgin. It must have been fun for the onlookers watching us trying to run to the bay our bus was leaving from. The abuse I took from Craig was terrible. Fortunately he was so out of breath he could hardly speak.

We got the bus no bother because it was running late. You've guessed it, we had to run from one bay to another in Elgin

Bus Station to get our next bus, the 33C to Lossiemouth. The 15 minute run to Lossiemouth gave Craig and me time to recover. Unfortunately he recovered his breath and gave me dog's abuse for not arranging the buses to run on time!

We got off the bus in the centre of town, and the first thing we saw was no pubs, and we hadn't passed any on the way into town, although there was a huge Airbase, which I had forgotten about. So we knew that if there were military people in town, there would be plenty of pubs somewhere. I was not concerned as it was Craig's idea to come here, so if there were no pubs, it was down to him. He said there were plenty and that he knew exactly where they were.

Unfortunately for me, he was right, and as we got to the harbour in brilliant sunshine, we found Craig's first pub in an idyllic setting overlooking the harbour.

Craig's 1st pub; *The Brander Arms;* Honest, I have nothing against Elgin. In fact we have spent many a happy hour enjoying ourselves in the many pubs of that fair town. I really like the place and the people. It is just that sometimes you need a bit of a change.

This was one of those times. I had to put my foot down. If we were going to visit the North of Scotland I wanted to see a different part of it.

John took a lot of convincing, mainly because he was too lazy to get the extra bus from Elgin.

It took a couple of months to bring him round to my way of thinking, that to see some really interesting pubs we should make the extra effort to get to Lossiemouth.

I'm sorry to have to admit that I probably told him a couple of small, whiteish lies to get my own way. For instance I may have indicated that the oldest pubs in the region were to be found in 'Lossie'. There is of course the chance that this information could be correct, though, personally I would be stunned if that proved to be the case. The important thing is, John believed it.

241

There was of course a price to pay for this change of scenery. For the first part of our day I was subjected to a fair amount of whining. It got worse with every bus we boarded. John had grudgingly agreed to do the planning for the trip and he was a bit worried since, on the outward leg we had to catch three different buses to get to our destination.

On paper this seemed easily achievable. There was always a good margin of time between buses which gave us plenty of leeway just in case any problems occurred with the timetable.

The problem was, buses travel on roads and not on paper. And sometimes they just don't travel fast enough. Not one of our buses left on time.

Our leeway disappeared entirely with the first bus and we were left playing catch-up all day. I was beginning to think it was a conspiracy. My mood wasn't helped much by my travelling companion doing a convincing impression of the Corporal Fraser character from 'Dad's Army'. I'm not saying that he spent all day whining about us being 'doomed', but it was pretty close.

Even when we got off the bus in Lossie he was going on about not seeing a single pub on the way in. I showed him the pub names on the internet but he still wasn't pleased.

They could all be shut he said. Just like the time I took him down to Creetown in Galloway and we discovered that there were no pubs open in the town. Honestly! That was four years ago and he is still going on about it.

Only when I dragged him round the corner of Shore Street and presented him with our first view of *The Brander Arms* did he stop giving me earache.

I had seen a couple of pictures of The Brander and it looked quite interesting. But seeing it for real was amazing. It is right beside the harbour wall. It is right beside the harbour and the fishing boats coming in have to pass by the pub window.

We actually watched a shrimp boat come in as we were standing at the bar. If the window had been open I could have chatted to the skipper as he passed by.

It was such a nice day that, had we not been working, we could have sat outside while we supped our drinks. But we were there to check out the pub, so we had to put up with sitting in a very comfortable pub, chatting to the licensee, Lynn Mitchell. That was no hardship as Lynn was a great laugh.

She produced a printed booklet which detailed a fair bit of the pubs history and talked us through it. Obviously she had clocked John's face when he saw all those big words on the pages of the booklet.

The Brander Arms

The Brander Arms, or at least the building it is in had once belonged to the local Laird. He had given the building to the harbour authority for their use. Later the harbour officials leased it out as a public house.

The records of the time are a bit unclear so the exact age of the pub is questionable. What is certain is that from 1870 there has been a public house within the building. That makes *The Brander Arms* at least 145 years old.

An article in the local newspaper of that year mentions the pub by name. Of course it is quite possible that the pub is much older than that, but no actual proof exists.

Lossiemouth was once a busy fishing port and Lynn told us that it was once possible to walk from one side of the harbour, dry footed, by stepping from one fishing boat to another as they lay tied up.

With the downturn in the fishing industry there are only a couple of boats left in the harbour.

Apparently, in the good old days there was a healthy trade in Black fish in and around the town. That's a reference to an early form of the black market and not the colour of the fish up for sale.

Under cover of darkness many tons of fish would be landed on the beaches outside of the harbour and sold on to customers, cutting out the middlemen and of course the taxman.

The Brander undoubtedly benefited from the fishing trade, legitimate and otherwise, as the skippers would use the pub as a place to pay their crews their hard-earned wages.

It doesn't take much imagination to work out what tired and thirsty fishermen would do when presented with a week's wages, in the middle of a cosy public house.

Lynn and Allan

While we were chatting, Lynn's husband, Allan, came in and we changed discussion topic from fishing to the influence on the town of the Air Force base.

It has provided a boost to the local economy, employing a lot of civilian contractors as well as Air Force personnel.

Allan works at the base, and unfortunately that was enough for John to constantly refer to him as Wing-Commander; he can be really embarrassing at times.

We asked our hosts if they could tell us of any other pubs in the town which were of a good age and they came up with one that I had never heard of. The Rock House didn't appear on any web site I had looked at. From what Allan told us it sounded like the kind of place we should be visiting.

What really made up our minds to go there was Allan's kind offer to drive us to the pub. A more suspicious person might interpret such an offer as a ploy to get shot of two old drunks who were cluttering up your bar, with the added bonus of inflicting them on one of your rivals. But we were certain that this wasn't the case here. Very certain indeed!

Leanne, Lynn and Allan's daughter, strolled into the pub and joined in the conversation. I was intrigued to hear that Leanne works at Gordonstoun, the famous public school. Since the place is jam-packed with the offspring of the rich and famous, not to mention self-appointed dictators and dodgy royal families, I asked her if she felt like spilling the beans on any of them.

I was quite willing to split the proceeds of any blackmail scam with her but she declined my offer. She did say that she had tried for a 'selfie' with a well-connected Middle Eastern gentleman, but his bodyguards had growled at her so she didn't bother with the photo.

It was time to move on. Our short stay in *The Brander Arms* had been very enjoyable. I was happy to find that it was probably the oldest pub in Lossiemouth. And John was happy to find that it fulfilled all the prerequisites of his dream pub. It doesn't do meals, there is no carpeting in the bar and, as far as we could tell, weans are not allowed in.

John's comments; *This was a lovely pub in a fabulous setting, especially on a good day. Lynn was great company and made us very welcome. Before we left, I asked Lynn's husband if* *he knew of a pub that might be older. Not only did he tell me that* The Rock House *pub might be older, but he said he would run us there. Makes you wonder if they were really nice people, or just wanted rid of us. Surely not!*

John's 1st pub; *Rock House Pub;* At first I thought this was a funny name for an old pub in a fishing village, but the Rock bit is nothing to do with modern (or not so modern) music, but because of an amazing tale that was to unfold. But more of that in a minute.

When Allan dropped us off, the first thing I noticed is that the pub is not old looking from the outside, and inside it is a bit like your living room. But these initial impressions do not tell the story of the real age and of past happenings.

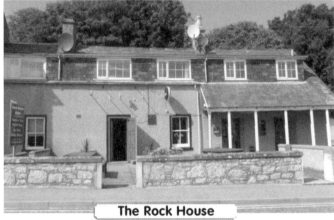

The Rock House

The owner, George Skelton, was not in, but the barmaid Amanda Stevens, who as worked in the place for a good few years was very helpful, as was Stevie, a local worthy who works at the Airbase. They told us that the original building, which is attached to the new one, and housed the pub, does in fact date back to the 1700s, but they said nobody knows exactly when it was opened. Amanda said the date is above the door on the old part of the building. The date was nowhere it be seen. Craig claimed that this meant that his pub was still the oldest.

246

But what they told us next was a fantastic story. *The Rock House* got it's name from the rocky cliff behind the original pub, which was built right into the rock. Now the entrance to the bar was down steps into a basement sort of bar, and from the back of the bar there was a secret entrance into a tunnel that went all the way to the Lighthouse, next to which there is a cave. Rumour has it that the tunnel was used to transport smuggled goods in the old days. How great a story is that? At least my pub is the oldest in town with a secret tunnel.

Stevie and Amanda

Amanda told us she thinks there are plans afoot to try and excavate the tunnel next year. There could be bodies and treasure to be discovered, or maybe not. Anyway, it's a brilliant story.

Although the present bar is not as old and atmospheric as *The Brander,* it is a good pub and well worth a visit. It could also be the oldest, but who knows!

We said our farewells and made our way back out into the sunshine to find our next pub, one which Stevie had told Craig about.

247

Craig's comments; I did enjoy chatting to Amanda and Stevie, and the beer was quite acceptable. The pub itself was not my kind of place. The bar area has a split level-and to me it is just an accident waiting to happen. In our short time there I very nearly managed a back flip down to the lower level while I was trying to take a photograph.

That would probably have made John's day but it could have had serious consequences for me. That camera cost a fortune.

Any claims to it being the oldest pub in Lossie do not stand up. This pub is not the original Rock House. It was situated in the building next door.

Therefore, once again, my first choice of pub proves to be *The Auldest Boozer in Toon.*

Craig's 2nd pub; *The Steamboat;* Going to *The Steamboat* was a bit of an afterthought on my part. But for once I actually made the right choice. Whereas *The Brander Arms* and *The Rock House* are fairly old pubs which have been modernised quite recently, *The Steamboat* still has the feel of a traditional, man's pub.

Man overboard at The Steamboat Inn

I would like to claim that I had thoroughly checked out the area and had chosen this pub on merit. The truth is however, I had no idea where the pub was or even if it was still open. The only reason we ended up in there was because I had seen it from the car when Allan had driven us past it on our way to *The Rock House.*

I liked the look of it and I especially liked the fact that it was only a hundred yards away from the bus stop we would be catching our next bus from.

Being in charge of the timetables meant John had been under pressure all day. Due to the tight schedule we needed to keep to it had been agreed that we would only visit two pubs in 'Lossie'. My insistence on visiting a third, *The Steamboat,* nearly tipped him over the edge.

With an eye on the timetable we struck up a conversation with the barmaid as soon as we got into the pub. Hazel Istance, our barmaid, is also the lease holder of the pub.

Hazel at the wheel of the Steamboat

Her pub is very bright and spacious. I think the décor is inspired by a nautical theme. There is a lot of varnished wood cladding and port hole shaped mirrors. Even the tables are themed. They are inlaid with marine navigational charts.

When he saw these, John suggested that it might be more helpful if at least one of the tables was inlaid with an easy to read bus timetable.

While talking to Hazel, her cousin, Gordon, who helps in the bar, came over. We had been talking about some of the daft things that happen in pubs and Hazel asked her cousin to tell us about some of the things he had done in The Steamboat. It seems that Gordon is a bit of a practical joker and has pulled a few corkers.

One joke he had been involved in concerned one of the girls in the bar. Patsy sells fresh eggs to the pub's customers. Finding the cartons of eggs unattended Gordon proceeded to boil them before putting them back in their boxes.

It caused a bit of a sensation around the town, especially around breakfast time the next morning.

Another plot he hatched was to slip a raw egg into the bottle of Corona Patsy was drinking one night in the pub. She didn't notice it until her last swig. Her reaction to this was not reported to us but I would imagine that there would be a few coarse words spoken. I was tempted to ask her if she got the 'yolk', but that might have been tempting fate.

It was Hazel's turn to get in on the fun. She told us about one of her regular customers who undergoes a change worthy of Jekyll and Hyde. He is normally a mild mannered 66 year old bachelor, who as far as anyone knows has never had a girlfriend. But when he has a bit of a session on the booze his character changes dramatically.

According to Hazel this mild mannered bloke then thinks stripping off will increase his chances with the ladies. So far they have always managed to stop him before he concludes his mating dance by whipping off his underpants. But it is only a question of time.

Before it was time to leave we made a bit of an effort to find out just how old The Steamboat was.

Nobody up at the bar seemed to know so we wandered over to talk to two of the pub's more mature patrons. Hugo Cameron

250

and Russell 'Compo' Fielding were sitting at a table over by the door. Unfortunately they couldn't help with dating the pub but we did get an interesting story from Compo.

I didn't catch his age, and didn't think it was very nice thing to keep asking, in case he thought I was suggesting he was around when this pub first opened. Suffice it to say, the old boy has been around for a fairly long time.

The Steamboat crew

He told us told us some tales of what life was like when he was a lad. It was an eye-opener. Times were tough back then. For example, Compo started his first job at the age of eight, when he would help the fishermen by tailing the prawns they had landed.

It would have been nice to sit and chat to the boys for a while but our time was up. We had to rush around the corner to catch our bus back to Elgin.

It had taken us about six and a half hours to get to Lossiemouth and in total we had only spent about two and a half hours in the pubs there. I think that we both enjoyed the trip, but knowing that it would be another eight and a half hours before we got home, we both agreed that we wouldn't be doing a day trip of this length again.

John's comments; This was another great bar overlooking the harbour and one of the best beaches I have ever seen. No idea if Craig ever found out how old it is, but it is a must to visit if you are in the town.

John; We left Lossiemouth about ten past four and got back to EK at 12.15 am the next morning. We were out for about 18 hours, three of which were spent in pubs. How about that for dedication to our art!

Find oor Auld Boozers

by Bus . . . .

From Glasgow's Buchanan Street Bus Station the Gold Bus number G10 whisks you in luxury up to Inverness. From there a Number 10 will take you the one hour journey to Elgin. Then it's a 15 minute journey on the 33C (C is for circular). It's a hell of a journey to do in a day, but an overnight in Elgin, or even Inverness at my brother's place would make it a great two day trip.

. . . . then by Boot

The Brander Arms
Get off the bus at James Square in Queen Street, turn left and walk down to the Harbour, you can't miss it.

The Rock House
Turn right when you leave the Brander, keep the water on your left, it's a ten minute walk if Allan doesn't give you a lift.

The Steamboat Inn
It's back down at the harbour front on the corner of Queen Street, and there you are.

Droving North

John; Craig had been going on for years about us travelling further from home. At first I thought he meant Edinburgh, but no, he wanted to do the Highlands and even the Islands.

If we agreed to do the far away islands-places like Lewis and Skye came to mind-we would have to stay overnight. Have any of you checked the prices of accommodation on these remote islands? You are cheaper going to Tenerife for a week, which I was doing anyway.

Craig was not to be put off, so a compromise was reached and we decided to stay on the mainland, but go further north. Craig had discovered that there was a place in Glen Coe called *Kings House Hotel* which has claims to being the oldest Inn in Scotland, and he maintained we should be going there anyway. So we started to plan this trip around Glen Coe and beyond.

We realised right away that to get buses to the places we were talking about was out of the question, on a day trip anyway, so what would we do?

It was my Kate who came up with a solution that would solve our problems. Why don't the four of us take the car and stay a couple of nights at the Ballachulish Hotel, who, as it just happened, were advertising a great deal for about £35.00 a night per person dinner, bed and breakfast. This is a magic price. Kate and I had visited it recently on a similar sort of deal, and the hotel and the food was brilliant. It's not the way we usually do our trips, but if we wanted to go as far as we were planning, I could see no alternative. Also, the wives promised not to join us in the bars we would visit, 'but just don't drink too much'. Wives know how to put the mockers on a good day out.

Checking the route to Glencoe, we would be passing *The Drovers,* near the top of Loch Lomond. This had to be our first port of call as it is a magic old Inn. We decided the *Kings House Hotel* would be next. I then said we would visit *The Clachaig Inn,* near the village of Glencoe. I have visited it a couple of times in the past and it has a great bar, which I reckoned might be older than Craig's *Kings House Hotel.*

After visiting these three Inns (pubs), we would book into our hotel. Our second day was to be spent visiting the Oldest pub in Fort William, which I was sure was the *Maryburgh Inn,* then it was onto the train to Mallaig to find the oldest pub there.

254

Using Google Earth, which on this occasion I must admit I did, there seemed to be three pubs in the town. One of them is called *The Steam Inn,* it sounds as if it is made for Craig and me.

Although doing this many pubs in two days sounds like a nightmare (no, not a massive piss-up), using the car, and having booked the hotel and even the train, meant that we should have no problems with our task. If we don't it will be the first time!

Kate had volunteered to do the driving after the work (us bevying) had started. We didn't have to worry about buses not turning up, or me screwing up the timetable reading.

Day One;

So with everything organised, the four of us set off for our three day/two night stay in the highlands.

Before we left, Craig agreed to let me have the first pub we would visit, *The Drovers,* as he wanted *The Kings House Hotel,* our second pub, as his.

It's a lovely run up to *The Drovers.* Once you get past the top of Dumbarton, Loch Lomond opens up in front of you and it's a beautiful run up the loch, though I've got to admit that the narrow bit of the road after Tarbet is a bit scary. As we were going round one of the many tight corners, a big lorry full of logs came the other way. It was almost brown trousers time, but I was magnificent at the wheel and we scrapped by.

Just after you pass Ardlui, *The Drovers* appears on the right hand side of the road. I was delighted as I knew Kate was driving from then on.

John's 1ˢᵗ pub; *The Drovers* is one of the most atmospheric-looking pubs in Scotland, outside and in. It looks really ancient and no two parts of the building are leaning the same way. One of the windows on the top right hand side of the building is not a real window-it is just painted to look like one.

As soon as we went in the front door, we saw the sign that told us that the pub had opened in 1701, which is very old. I'm sure

Craig realised that this might be older than his choice, *Kings House Hotel*, so he was like a 'Bear with a sore heid', as the photograph shows. But his mood only lasted for a few moments as he had to admit this was a great looking pub. It's the kind of pub we like, old and dirty looking, although this image is intentional as the place is clean, well as clean as it can be with two open fires blasting away.

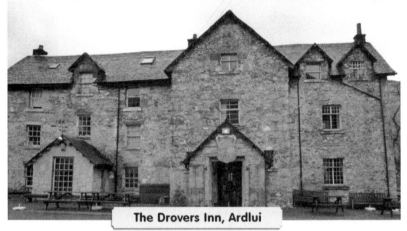

The Drovers Inn, Ardlui

The walls are covered with ancient-looking paintings, books, and wild animals that have died crashing their heads through the pub walls, or that's how it looks. The floor is all over the place and everything looks as if it is on its last legs. It's a fantastic pub. But as you know, we're here to get some background on the pub and to try and find out it the date claimed is correct.

I spoke to one of the kilted barmen, Greg Watson, who showed me an ancient cutting on the wall which proved not only that the pub was the age it claimed, but that one of the regulars was none other than one of Scotland's greatest heroes, Rob Roy. Some of his battles against the English were very close to the pub, and I suppose he came in before the battle for a bit of Dutch Courage, and after the battle for a couple to celebrate the victory, or possibly drown his sorrows.

Now, my version of this piece of history might not be as factually accurate as Craig or most other serious people might want to portray it, but it's more or less what I think happened.

Greg was very helpful, and after another couple of drinks, he showed me a very sad notice on the wall which told the story of a wee girl who drowned in the stream behind the pub. This happened over a hundred years ago, but her ghost still appears in the bed of room six, up the stairs from the bar. Some people have sworn to have been wakened during the night by a cold torso rubbing against them, I can sympathise! This sad story brought me back down to earth and I had to have another drink to drown my sorrows. It worked.

A wee bit tipsy, John finds someone to listen to him

Another story is of a family of Highlanders who had been thrown out of their croft by the English Landlord. They were heading south looking for work and one evening in a terrible snow storm, they all died of the cold. This happened just behind *The Drovers*. I asked Greg if any happy stories ever happened; 'yes', he replied, 'but they are not as interesting as the bad ones for the tourists'.

This Inn is a must for all true Scot's to put on their Bucket List, and there are bedrooms up the stairs for the people who are no feart of ghosties. We had another before the women dragged us out. To be fair to Kate, she didn't remind me not to drink too much. We left with Kate behind the wheel and we headed up through Crianlarich. Well, that's what I thought, but the local council have built a bypass which means you don't go through the wee town. This will probably mean some small business going under, but it saved us all of one and a half minutes on our trip!

The run up towards Glen Coe is magic, although the bit of the road at the end of Rannoch Moor must be a bit dreich on a bad day.

Craig's comments; I liked The Drovers Inn. It's exactly how a country pub should be, except for all the other tourists and people stopping off for something to eat and a soft drink.

Craig's 1ˢᵗ pub, It is quite possible to get a bus to *The Kings House* in Glencoe, but it is probably not advisable. I think there may be a bus every other hour but, because of the distances involved, it would be a very limited visit.

That is to say, the bus you would need to get back might not leave you very much time for a relaxing pint or two. Since we were travelling by car we had no such limitation, although having Irene and Kate along with us could well put a bit of a spoke in our drinking wheel.

Another point to ponder for the would-be traveller is the fact that the A82 in winter is not a road you can rely on. Even in what passes for a reasonable Scottish summer the climate can turn gey dreech at an alarming speed.

As we turned off the main road and headed towards the hotel one of the girls pointed out the very life-like animal statues which had been placed on the small grassy area next to the car park. It was only when we got out of the car that we realised that just how life like these statues were.

Glencoe's oldest watering hole

The small herd of deer looked completely unfazed by our arrival, but I did notice that John was not quite as casual as these wild creatures. I think I was the only person to clock that he made a point of keeping the girls between him and the big beasties.

Since we were not at *The Kings House* just to enjoy ourselves it had been agreed that the ladies would adjourn to the comfort of the lounge while us workers headed round to the Climber's bar.

It really is a spectacular setting for a pub, although the door to the bar is very close to a fast-flowing burn. I said to John that if we were ever to become regulars in there the owners would have to invest in some fairly heavy duty fencing to avoid losing a couple of well-oiled veterans to a watery grave.

We joked about the possibility of some of these hardy types who climb up sheer rock faces using nothing but a blunt ice-axe and their mammy's washing line coming to a sticky end in the burn after a wee session in the bar. It turns out that the proprietors of the hotel do worry about that possibility and are always warning their patrons to take care when leaving the bar. Nothing buggers up the tourist trade like a bit of unintentional white water body-surfing.

259

Kerrie and Jessie keeping warm in Glencoe

The bar was exactly what I expected of a place aimed at climbers and walkers. In fact I don't think it could have been better laid out if it had been built as a movie set. There is a lot of stone and a fair bit of untreated wood and plenty of rucksacks, ropes and those jaggy things climbers wear on their boots.

There was not the merest hint of any frills or cushioned seating. Well that's the way I remember it anyway. The downside to all this outdoorsiness was that both of us were painfully aware that we were a good 30 years off the boil to be part of the scene.

Up at the rugged but functional bar we ordered a couple of drinks and tried, without the least bit of success, to look like tough mountain folk. Any credibility we might have had disappeared entirely when John asked for a slice of lemon for his vodka and soda.

Our barmaid, Kerrie Vango, had the most curious Scottish accent I had ever heard. I was still going on about it when she told me that she was actually from Essex and had only been in Scotland for a few months.

We got chatting to a young couple, Gill Cairney and partner John Toms, who had come in for a meal. Like the bar, their meal looked really good, in a rough hill-bothy sort of a way. Thinking they were part of the outdoorsy crowd I gave them the benefit of my hillwalking patter. Of course I didn't bother to explain to them that all my first-hand knowledge was 3 decades out of date. I shouldn't have bothered. It turned out that John had just completed the 282 Munroes. They were unlikely to be impressed by my ancient wanderings.

John went up the hill - Jill didnae

At this point the proprietor, Jessie Cattanach, appeared behind the bar, and the level of fun and laughter rose accordingly. Jessie is very proud of her hotel and we could only agree with her that it was an exceptional place to visit.

She asked us about our travels and even offered to drive us to our next stop, once we had had a decent wee drink. I have of course heard of Highland hospitality, but up until then I had thought it was a bit like The Loch Ness Monster: much talked about but never encountered.

Anyway we settled down for a wee session in the knowledge that Irene and Kate were quite happy sitting through in the much plusher lounge.

While we sipped our refreshments Jessie filled us in on the history of *The King's House*. *The Kings House* was built in the 17th century. It got its present name from the time it was used as barracks for King George's troops after the defeat of the Jacobite's in 1746.

Although it is now a warm and welcoming place to visit that has not always been the case. Dorothy Wordsworth, sister of the famous poet, was far from impressed with the facilities at *The Kings House*.

In 1803 she wrote a scathing report on the hotel worthy of one of those rants you read on Tripadvisor. She complained that the place was manky, the sleeping arrangements a bit suspect and the food inedible. Fortunately things have improved since those days.

In the past the Kings House Hotel has provided shelter for many drovers as they moved their cattle down from the Isle of Skye to the markets in Falkirk.

Due to the unique geography of the area a large dam was constructed near the hotel. The building of the dam provided some much needed employment for the men of the Highlands, but like most large projects there was a high price to pay for its completion.

After a hard shift dam building, many of the labourers would make the long trek across open moorland to enjoy a few well-earned drinks at *The Kings House*. Unfortunately quite a few of them never made it back to their work camp. A combination of booze and freezing temperatures meant that many of these men died out on the hills surrounding the hotel.

I would imagine that two or three probably ended up in that burn as well.

While we had been chatting I became aware of the 'Specials Board' next to the bar. I've never actually tasted venison; there was never much call for it in the mining village I grew up in. And I can certainly say that making such prime meat into burgers would never have occurred to anyone making up the filled rolls in the pubs down there.

The chalk drawing of the burgers on the board was fine but the set of antlers nailed just above it got me thinking about those docile 'statues' outside.

262

On our way back to the car I noticed that there were fewer deer wandering around. The explanation for this might be quite innocent; the deer are free to wander about after all.

John's comments; The most amazing thing for me was seeing about 20 Deer just sitting or standing on the bit of lawn outside the Hotel. They came towards us as we got out the car. I thought this was brilliant until I saw that Venison Burgers were the speciality of the Hotel. I shooed them away when we left.

No complaints about the bar, it was great. As I expected, we were the only non-climbers in the bar, but they were all friendly. Only worry for me is that I think Craig has proved that this is the oldest bar, on this trip anyway. Who cares!!

John's 2ⁿᵈ Pub; The Clachaig Inn. I had visited this Inn several times in the past, so I knew how to get there and how good a bar it had, but was it the oldest? We would soon find out.

Before we went in, I pointed out the site of Hagrid's house in the Harry Potter films. There are other areas within sight of the Inn that were also used in the films; Craig was less than impressed.

The bar is round the back of the Hotel, and the entrance is not very welcoming, but inside is something else. It is a fantastic bar, with the wooden tables and chairs, an open fire, and hundreds of different beers on tap. This again did not impress Craig as all he ever drinks is Lager.

To be fair, the place was fairly empty and lacked a bit of atmosphere. 'Steely', our bearded barman, told us that all the climbers were on the hills and would be in later. The other barman, William, tried, without success, to find out exactly how old the place was. The closest he could get was over 300 years. Now that's pretty old to me, but Craig claimed that it comes behind *The Kings House* and maybe even behind *The Drovers*, my first pub, which, by my reckoning, is 314 years old.

263

Steely protects his horde of booze from John

Although it was quiet, we talked to a nice climbing couple, who told us that they had got engaged in the bar of *The Clachaig*. I told them that that was lovely. Mind you, I couldn't help wondering that if after the wedding, the groom told the bride to get the boots and crampons on for a surprise honeymoon.

Craig's Comments; *: The Clachaig Inn is a huge barn of a place. It would probably have been a better experience if the place had been busy. As it was, we were alone for most of our time in* The Clachaig.

This included time for a light lunch, because of the girls insisting we needed to eat something if we were 'going to be drinking all day'.

It would have been nice to see a bit of a crowd in the place, as by my reckoning, this pub could probably accommodate a couple of hundred mountaineering types.

Incidentally, the Glencoe Mountain Rescue team was established by Hamish MacInnes and a group of climbers in this very pub.

It is probably a great place to visit if you are a member of a large group of walkers or climbers, but I didn't fancy it at all. I've no idea how old it is and to be honest I couldn't care less, I had already found the oldest pub in the area.

John; Feeling no plain, but having done a lot of research, the girls caught up with us in the bar, dragged us out and Kate drove us the short journey to our hotel, *The Ballachulish.*

Craig and I thought that since the hotel had a bar, we should go in right away and check how old was. 'You've had enough', was the loud message from the girls, who dragged us up to our rooms for a wee sleep before we met up for dinner and more drink.

Day Two;

Our memory of yesterday slowly returned over breakfast, helped by the girls reminding us of how drunk we were. I've said it before; the wives know how to ruin the enjoyment of a good piss up.

Kate said she would drive us to Fort William, as she reckoned I would still be well over the drink driving limit. I wonder if I'm ever under it?

We parked at the station, and Craig and I headed for our next pub while the girls did a bit of shopping. We had only an hour and a bit before our train, so we wanted to be in the pub at eleven sharp. Again, I said I would take the first pub of day two.

John's 1st pub; *The Maryburgh Inn.* We had visited this pub about three books ago, but we had to do it for this book as I found out (on the web, would you believe) that this is the oldest pub in Fort William. For those of you who did not read the previous book which featured this pub, this will all be new. For the rest of you of my age group and memory who did read the book, it will all be new to you too!

The pub is found halfway down the High Street on the left hand side of the street going away from the Train or Bus Stations. It is easy to miss as the entrance is a small gate which leads to a set of steps taking you down a dark alley. I remember being scared of going down the steps the first time. It was only because we had a good few already that I was brave enough. Today, it was eleven o'clock and I was sober. I remembered that it was a great pub inside, so down and in we went.

I was hoping Geoff and Gillian, who were running the bar last time, would be in. Unfortunately Geoff was off with a broken shoulder, and Gillian was also off, but I didn't find out why. Luckily Lillian, the Scrubber, was in and we had a good time talking to her again. The big lad behind the bar was called Martin Cameron. He told us he was usually the bouncer, but was helping out behind the bar as he is qualified.

Exactly what he was qualified at I wasn't sure. I could believe the Bouncer bit, but he looked almost too big to fit in behind the bar. The fact that he was wearing a Superman Top made him look unusual. Anyway, he was over to us in a single bound to ask what we were drinking and to find out what two oldies were doing down in the dunny early in the drinking day.

When I told him that we were looking for the oldest pub in town, he made some discouraging remark about *The Maryburgh* being a fairly new pub. I asked him if he was the mild mannered Clark Kent at the moment. He told me he was, so I said he was talking mince. This pub looks a thousand years old and has a wishing well in the middle of it for goodness sake, I told him. He was not impressed and we changed the subject and spent the rest of our visit talking to Superman, and a mad local who may have been called James (although I doubt it) about politics.

Today was the day of the General Election so we had a great laugh at the local MP Charles Kennedy's expense. The poor man lost his seat later that day, and has now died; we did say he was a nice block, so I don't feel too bad.

This may, or may not be the oldest pub in Fort William, but in my opinion it is one of the best places in town to spend an hour or two dropping coins down the well and wishing you were in Majorca. It's a great old pub. But is it the oldest. I was a bit worried about the amount of time Craig was talking to an old worthy trying to find out about the pub, or was he?

All to soon we had to leave and walk along the High Street to catch our train to Mallaig.

Craig's Comments; He might not know much but by god he knows how to pick them. John's choice for the oldest pub in Fort William, The Maryburgh Bar *doesn't have a lot going for historically speaking. Although he continues to insist he was right, deep down he knows full well that the pub is only about 50 years old.*

I know this because the barman and all the customers told us so. It was quite humorous to watch him try to convince the locals that he knew more about their pub than they did.

By the time we were getting ready to leave I think they felt sorry for us both. Sorry for John's obvious mental health problems and sorry for me because I had to put up with him.

Craig's 1ˢᵗ pub of day two; *The Steam Inn.* The journey from Fort William to Mallaig turned out to be rather interesting, which surprised me greatly. Unless you are actually trying to catch the ferry to The Isle of Skye there is no real reason why you should be on the train up to Mallaig.

That is unless you are a Harry Potter fan. The train goes over the Glenfinnan Viaduct, which apparently featured in these films. I only mention this because of a conversation I overheard on the train.

As a service to the tourists, the train stops when it gets to the middle of the viaduct. A young American couple behind me were discussing the magnificent scenery.

The boy said to his girlfriend that he wasn't sure whether or not the viaduct had been built for the film, but he did know that the statue down by the shore of the loch was put there to commemorate the making of the films.

I toyed with the idea of setting this American genius straight about Bonnie Prince Charlie, his statue and the Jacobite Rebellion of 1745.

Another option, and my personal favourite, was to slap some sense into the silly bugger, no matter how long that might take.

In the end I remembered that the girls were travelling with us and might frown on such behaviour so I settled for slowly shaking my head in frustration.

Once in Mallaig the girls headed off in search of a good café giving John and myself no option but to stop off in *The Marine Bar* to get our bearings.

The Marine Bar is a very basic, no frills pub. It had probably last been done up in the 1960s and it hasn't occurred to anyone to do it up again. In fact it was exactly what I had expected to find on the road to the Isles. And of course I fully expected the other pubs in Mallaig to be of a similar standard. I couldn't have been more wrong.

We asked a couple of the guys in the bar which of the town's pubs was the oldest and, after a heated debate, the consensus of opinion was that *The Steam Inn* was the, pub we were looking for.

From the outside *The Steam Inn* looked like a really traditional Scottish pub, although it did seem a wee bit on the well-kept side for my liking. I put this down to Mallaig being a bit of a tourist town.

My worries about the pub went off the scale when we went inside. It had been transformed from an ordinary boozer into an ultra-modern 'yuppie' palace. I was not impressed.

It was hard to believe that all of that stainless steel and exotic hard-wood fittings, not to mention the leather couches (COUCHES… in a pub!), could be part of the oldest pub in any town.

That is not to say that *The Steam Inn* is not a good pub, because it is. It's just that the décor is not to my taste. Then again I don't suppose that I'm the type of customer the owners were thinking of when they renovated the place.

"Lets get steamin"

But as we always say, it's the bar staff who can make or break a pub. Fortunately for *The Steam Inn*, and us, our barmaid, Steff Milligan, makes the pub very welcoming.

Steff told us that she was pretty sure that this pub really was the oldest one in town, but just to be sure she decided to get a second opinion.

The pub is owned by her family and the head of that family, her granny, was upstairs taking a bit of a break. So Steff phoned her to ask about the pub's history. I think she would probably have come down to talk to us, but I had made a mistake. I had mentioned that we liked to take pictures of the people we talked to in the pubs we visit. Apparently Steff's gran was not keen on making an appearance in our book.

John mentioned something to the effect that people of a certain age can be a bit funny about meeting strangers. He followed up this cliché by asking Steff what age the old lady was. He was less than thrilled to be told that the granny, or Granny Lala as she is known to everyone, was in fact a couple of years younger than he was. I laughed, a wee bit.

Steff serves up the firewater in The Steam Inn

We never did get the date of the pub's first opening but we did learn that The Steam Inn had originally been called The Central Bar. I can understand why that was changed as the pub is nowhere near the centre of town. Quite why they changed it from a traditional boozer into a trendy bar is more puzzling.

I doubt if anyone from outside Scotland will get the joke in the pub's new name. But I have no doubt that it has started many a conversation among the many tourists who find their way into the pub.

While at the bar enjoying a rather decent pint of lager I got talking to an old chap who told me he used to be a ferry boat captain. I had told him about hearing the mad Americans on the train up to Mallaig and it turned out that he had a similar story to tell.

A middle aged American woman, who had been on his ferry the day before, came over to talk to him as he guided the ferry into the harbour. She pointed to the pier and asked him why there was a lot less water there today than there had been the day before.

Since he didn't fancy explaining the mechanics high and low tides he simply replied, "Aye that happens quite often around here".

Before we could leave the pub someone brought up the subject of pub ghosts. I tried very hard to steer the conversation away from this, my least favourite topic, but it was too late.

It seems that a young girl died from TB in the pub building many years ago. Steff claims that the ghost of this small child has been seen wandering around place at night. Although for some reason she hasn't been seen for some time now.

I suggested that the wean, like some of the regulars, didn't recognise the place after all the modernisation and had moved on.

We really enjoyed our short visit to this pub, but I think we both would have preferred to see the place before the great renovation-back when Granny Lala was a young girl and John was still an old guy.

But as they say you can't stop progress. You can only whinge on about it at great length. We certainly do.

John's Comments; *This is not the type of pub we like. It was at one time, but has now been changed into a fancy restaurant with fancy prices for the tourists. The bar area is very small.*

Having said that, the staff maketh the bar, and the barmaid Steff was great company and made us very welcome. Anyone going to Mallaig will probably have the missus with them, so this would be an ideal place for the better half.

John's 2ⁿᵈ pub of day two; *The Clachan.* This bar was a bit further up the hill and only about 100 yards from *The Steam Inn.* Although it has also been done up recently, you can still imagine you are in a real bar, apart from the tables serving food and the sparkly bar-top.

It's a very nice pub, and the owner, Cameron Boyd, and the barmaid Yvone Dempster made us very welcome. When I enquired about the history of the pub, Cameron showed us photos showing the street with and without the pub in it. The photos proved that the pub had been built around the 1900s, so *The Steam Inn* is the oldest pub in town. This round to Craig.

The Clachan

I got into conversation with two locals, Catherine and Angus. They were great company and apart from the stories they were telling me, showed me a huge glass bell-shaped container on the bar which was full of homemade scones. These were the biggest scones I have ever seen. Ships have been anchored to smaller structures. These scones, and the 'Harry Potter' viaduct you cross on the train journey, are the two sights not too be missed on a trip to Mallaig.

As an interesting tailpiece to this riveting tale, I found out that Cameron is from Blantyre, and was at High Blantyre Primary School when Kate was teaching there. He was only a 5 or 6 years old then but he thinks he remembers Kate. We didn't have time to get Kate back to the pub as we had to leave for the train back to Fort William, but I told him he would still recognise Kate, even though it was over 40 years ago. Good-eh!

Yvonne and Cameron-The Clachan Crew

Craig's comments; The Clachan Inn; *A very spacious pub and well laid out. But once again we found that it had recently been modernised. Does no one in the highlands like the authentic look of an old time Scottish boozer? This is not, as you might expect, a reference to John, but is a plea to leave some of our pubs un-gentrified. Just like* The Marine Bar *in fact.*

Irene and Kate - oor Roadies!

John; Back in Fort William, Kate did the necessary and drove us back to the hotel where we had a wee rest and then enjoyed another great night in the Ballachulish Hotel. Still have no idea how old the bar is.

Find oor Auld Boozers

The Drovers Inn
You go up the A82, past Tarbet, and you'll find it on the right hand side of the road, just past Ardlui.

The Kingshouse Hotel
You carry on up the A82, past the edge of the Rannoch Moor, a real bleak looking place, and the Hotel is on your right. It's signposted and you can see it from the main road.

The Clachaig Inn
Get back onto the A82 heading for Glen Coe. You cut off onto the old road to the village of Glen Coe. Again it's well signposted. The Inn is a couple of minutes on the left.

The Maryburgh Inn
It's on the High Street, the left hand side if you are walking away from the bus station. It's a wee narrow entrance down a dark set of stairs. But worth the effort to find it.

The Steam Inn
The best, and most scenic way to arrive in Mallaig is going by train from Fort William. Turn left out of the station, walk past *The Marine* bar, first left, and its about 50 yards on the left.

The Clachan Inn
Turn right out of *The Steam Inn* and *The Clachan* is about 100 yards up the hill on the other side of the road.

East Kilbride

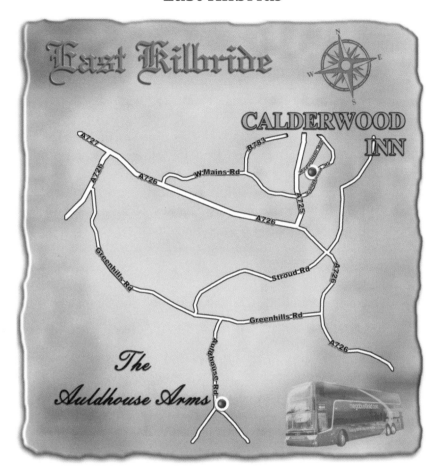

John; Our home town. We had to cover it in the book or we will get a slagging from our pals and book buyers in the town. East Kilbride is one of the biggest towns in Scotland. I'm not sure. It might even be a city, but I don't think so.

Although building of the new town did not start until 1947, the same year as the birth of the great, and legendary author, John (me) Mackay, the village of East Kilbride has been in existence for hundreds of years.

Are there any pubs in the old town, or even new town, that are really old. Our challenge, as always, was to find out. I won't bore you with how we got to EK.

E.K's oldest pub: Now, as you all should know, *The Montgomerie Arms* in the Village claims, with justification, to be the oldest, and it is a pub we have visited hundreds of times, and have written about in previous epics. This time, we decided to miss out on *The Monty*, and try and find the oldest pub in EK (and surrounding area) that is not *The Monty*.

For the record, I can officially confirm that it is the oldest pub in E.K. I believe it was built around 1656. I hope that is correct. It is also a brilliant bar and lounge bar and can be found in the village next to the old church, just look for the steeple and you're there. So in reality, we are looking for the second and third oldest pubs.

As is the tradition, Craig got to pick the first pub to be visited, the one he reckoned was the oldest.

Craig's 1st pub: *The Auldhouse Arms;* It is quite rare for me to be able to write about a pub I consider to be my 'local'. But for the last ten years or so I have been knocking back the odd pint or two in the bar of *The Auldhouse Arms*, which is situated in the village of the same name just outside East Kilbride.

To be more precise, every Tuesday night, when not out and about gathering material for our books or being desperately ill, I can be found enjoying my evening up there.

Tuesday might seem an unusual day of the week to be travelling out of town to a country pub, but *The Auldhouse* has attractions beyond really good beer. Tuesday nights are music nights up at Auldhouse.

A six piece band playing a mixture of traditional Scottish, Folk and Blues music make it a rare night in the bar. I would imagine that it is one of the busiest country pubs in Scotland; on Tuesday nights anyway.

Although the pub is going through a bit of a revamp at the moment it will always be a traditional Scottish country inn.

Over the years it has changed a little but has never lost any of its character. At one time the then owner was considering up the bar area by removing a small snug which had been built at the back of the room.

Knowing that some of his customers would be less than pleased if he simply went ahead and ripped out the old structure, he decided to share the blame. By getting the bar patrons to vote on whether it should stay or go, he not only avoided any flak from the traditionalists in the pub, but may well have kick started all the nonsense we are subjected to nowadays in TV shows like the X-Factor. I hope he is proud of himself!

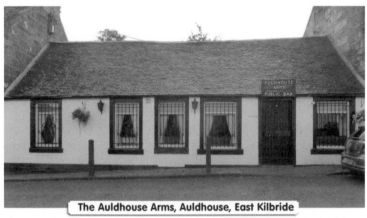

The Auldhouse Arms, Auldhouse, East Kilbride

In a close run contest 58 per cent of the voting public agreed with the gaffer's plan to change the bar. Some of the losing faction alleged a dirty tricks campaign had been in operation, with suggestions of 'Sooking up tae the boss' being muttered.

Fortunately no one has ever decided to alter the bar and its gantry. That would be a crime. The public bar gantry is about a hundred years old and is the only one of its kind that I have ever come across in all of my travels. And I have seen a fair few pubs in my time.

The quarter circle mahogany gantry contains two full size upright spirit barrels as well as some copper and pewter measuring pots. The dark wood of the bar matches the panelling which continues right around the pub walls.

The original pub is over 200 years old. Starting off as a single story building, over the years it has grown. Incorporating buildings to the left and right of the bar it is now many times the size of its humble beginnings. According to a few people we talked to, the original owner was a lady by the name of Granny Gilchrist.

The unique quarter circle gantry

Apart from serving a more than decent pint of beer *The Auldhouse* does a rather good line in food. We have often had a bar meal in the place and even the occasional meal in the restaurant attached to the pub.

When visiting pubs we usually ask some of the regulars for a story or two. I had thought about supplying a story or two of my own, given my near 'regular' status.

Tuesday night is music night at The Auldhouse

But there was a major stumbling block to that ever happening. It is called self-preservation. I intend to enjoy quite a few more Tuesday nights up at Auldhouse so I'll be spilling the beans on nobody, especially not the girls who gather behind our table louping about the place singing and dancing with nothing but white wine to keep them going.

Instead I'll settle for telling a wee story about one of the pubs oldest customers. On the day of our 'official' visit there were only a couple of blokes in the bar. One of them turned out to be John Clark.

Old John told us that he was 91 years and three months old and that he came up to Auldhouse every week day for his lunch. I don't know if it is one of those lunches arranged for pensioners or it was just something he liked to do, but he certainly enjoys the food.

Old John was full of praise for the food, especially since the new owner Pauline O'Donnell had taken over both the pub and the restaurant 'The Lost Lamb'.

Inevitably the subject of age came up. John was keen to know exactly what old John did to get to his great age. The auld fella said that was easily answered. All we had to do to get to his age was to make sure that we didn't drink any more than four pints of beer a day. He might not be a qualified physician, but that sounded like the kind of prescription we both could deal with; most of the time.

Fraser and Paul are a glass act

Of course he also mentioned that he had never married and we wondered if that too was a factor in his long and happy life.

We concluded our visit to *The Auldhouse Ar*ms by doing a bit of quality control on a few more beers. They passed with flying colours!

Thankfully Irene arrived to take us home just in time to stop us from over-staying our welcome.

John's comment's; It was no surprise to me that Craig picked The Auldhouse. *It is on the outskirts of the town, and I am not sure if it can be classed as an EK pub. Craig assured me that it is in the postal code district of EK. Sounds like a get-out to me, but it is a favourite of Craig's and there was no stopping him. Mind you, it would have been a taxi or a three mile walk if Craig's Irene had not driven us there and back, what a woman. She really believes we are working!*

As he has mentioned, it is probably the oldest pub that is not The Monty *and it is a brilliant bar. The only fault with the pub is that if you are not one of the 25 or so residents who live in the village, it is a taxi home, even after one pint, and who wants one pint!*

Craig, who is a regular, is a bit concerned that the new owner is making changes to the bar area that are maybe not to his liking. Curtains and things are being put up, chairs are being stuffed, and some of the old nick-nacks are being taken down. At least something is being done to update the pub, unlike some others which are struggling to stay open.

But if you are one of the thousands of tourists who come to Scotland to visit Edinburgh, Loch Lomond, or East Kilbride, the Auldhouse *is a must to visit, a great pub with a brilliant restaurant at the back.*

John's 1ˢᵗ pub: *The Calderwood Inn:* I reckoned that this must be one of the oldest pubs in town. Although it's on the edge of the new town, it's still part of the village, so it should be old.

It's hard to believe, or maybe not, but we got off at the wrong bus stop and had a longer walk than we should have. This started Craig with his moaning. After over 40 years in the town, I still manage to mess up.

The Calderwood Inn, East Kilbride

281

The Calderwood is the sort of pub Craig and I love, if it was closer to our houses, it would definitely be our local. It's a traditional man's pub. Children are not encouraged, no food is served, except on occasions, dogs are welcomed, and the staff is the best in town.

The pub is family owned and the manager Pamela Steel made us very welcome. She was not sure exactly how old the pub was, so she phoned several people in the trade to find out.

Seemingly, the pub called *The Calderwood* started up in 1956, this had me worried that my pub would end up being the newest pub in town, but further research revealed that it had been *The Coach House Inn* before, and been in existence for hundreds of years, that's good enough for me.

Further confirmation of the pub's history was given by an old regular called Ian, who wandered in during our discussion about it's age. 'How old is the pub', Pamela asked him. 'Older than me', was his instant comeback. You canny beat EK humour.

Pamela told us that it is a great football supporter's pub, and both Rangers and Celtic coaches leave from the pub every Saturday, or whenever the games are played nowadays, and that there is never any trouble between the fans.

She was proud to tell us that many famous people have been born in Calderwood. Lorrain Kelly and Ally McCoist are just two of the several.

Pamela kept us amused and amazed with her stories of things that happened during her time behind bars. Attempted murder and attempted rape were two things she witnessed in a pub in a very rough area of Kilmarnock. I can't mention the name of it, although Craig was a regular when he lived there. for a while. Mind you, the attempted rape could have been worse if the man had not managed to fight off the women. Another bar she worked in in Cumbernauld had no windows as they kept getting shot out. Some place Cumbernauld, eh!

When Craig mentioned, (several times), that he was building a bar in his shed, Pamela was kind enough to give him glasses and other memorabilia to put in it.

Pamela, the manager

To soon it was time to leave, so it was with a heavy heart, and light wallet, that we staggered out into the sunshine and walked back home via the village, stopping for a swift one on the way. So ended a brilliant day out in EK. Who needs Edinburgh and Loch Lomond when there are places like what we visited today on our doorstep.

Craig's comments: The Calderwood Inn is a fine example of a traditional village pub. In the days before the creation of East Kilbride new town Calderwood was a stand-alone village.

Now incorporated into the big town it still retains the feeling of a small village. And fortunately for those of us who like the odd pint of beer in old fashioned surroundings the Inn has changed very little over the years. Long may it continue!

Find oor Auldest Boozers

by Bus . . . .

There are plenty of buses that take you from Glasgow to East Kilbride.

The No. 18 goes up through Bridgetown, Rutherglen and Burnside.

The No. 6 goes through the Gorbals, Queens Park, Clarkston and Busby.

The No. 21 goes through Kings Park and Castlemilk.

For those of you bus pass holders with money to burn, £1.20 will get you a return on the train which drops you in the village.

. . . . then by Boot

The Auldhouse Arms

It's not easy. A three mile walk from the bus station or a fiver in a taxi. I don't know of any buses that go to Auldhouse.

The Calderwood Inn

From the EK Bus Station, the No. 6, 18 or 201 will get you to walking distance in a couple of minutes. If you want to walk all the way, just go into the village, turn right at *The Village Inn,* which is owned by the same family as own *The Calderwood,* and it's a 5 minute walk to the pub.

The newest pub in Scotland

John; This book has been all about the oldest pubs in Scotland. But now I am going to tell you all about Scotland's newest pub. And what a beauty it is!

The Stoat Inn

The first thing you should know is that it is not a Pub in the traditional manner. It is a Shed, but what a shed. The story that follows is the dramatic, and traumatic story of the trials and hardships Craig has gone through to complete, what many people have said is the finest pub in Scotland, bar none.

Some of these hardships and trials would have finished a lesser man, but Craig is of Auchinleck stock-made of Iron. Nothing, not even a blazing inferno in the middle of the night would stand in his way of achieving his lifelong ambition-a boozer in his back garden. Here in words and pictures is the story of *The Stoat Inn.*

In the Spring of this year, Craig told me about his dream of having a pub in his garden, not a shed with a bit of a pub in the corner of it, but a complete newly built shed made into a pub.

285

Craig had mentioned this dream to me a few times in the last year or two, usually after a good few pints, so I never took it too seriously. But in March, I think it was, he said that he had funds in hand and was going ahead with his dream. The first thing I asked him (well the first after 'are you aff your heid'), was what did Irene think about it. Craig said she was all for it, although he did tell her the main reason for the new structure was to do his writing, as well as a small area for a bar!

As you will see in the photographs, it's a bar. End of story. But what a story it is to tell.

About three nights after the erection of the shed, hooligans set fire to the bins in his garden. Unfortunately, the bins were next to the shed, and it was set ablaze.

Too close for comfort

Craig was awakened by the shouts of his neighbours, and raced out into his garden. The sight that confronted him was a vision of Hell. The bins and the Shed were ablaze. Now most people would have given up the ghost, but not Craig. He immediately started fighting the fire with buckets of water, immune to the pain from the lacerations on his bare feet.

He could hear the Fire Brigade approaching, and managed, through sheer determination and willpower, to keep the fire under control.

The scene that met Craig and Irene in the morning was a devastated garden and badly burned shed. Would Craig give in?

No. His dream would not die. With the drive and energy of a man half his age, he cleaned the mess, sanded and replaced bits of the shed and vowed *The Stoat Inn* would rise like a Phoenix from the Ashes.

The shed was sanded, varnished and painted on the outside. The inside was lined with insulation, the walls panelled, painted and finished with beams and skirting. Electricity was wired in from the house.

John paints himself into a corner

Craig built the bar with his bare hands, and made a Gantry which is a match for any of the 550 pubs we have visited in our travels.

The end product

If any vandals approach, let me warn them. There is also more security around and inside *The Stoat Inn* than there is in the new jail in Peterhead. So be warned!

Craig's Comment: *I agree with everything he said.*

Welcome to the Stoat Inn

How to get there;-I'm no' telling you!